An Introduction to
IT PROJECT FINANCIALS -
budgeting, cost management and
chargebacks

An Introduction to
IT PROJECT FINANCIALS -
budgeting, cost management and chargebacks

Michael Gentle

Contents

Introduction

"It's difficult to get a man to understand something when his salary depends on his not understanding it...." (Upton Sinclair)

The IT budget in the average company represents anywhere from 2% to 8% of revenue (2010 State of the CIO annual survey) and up to 50% of capital spend (Gartner), and it covers everything from software and hardware to development and support. With that type of money, one would logically think that the average IT staffer has, if not a sound knowledge of IT financials, at least a reasonable understanding of the basics, so that he can see how his daily activities contribute to these numbers.

Unfortunately, this is rarely the case. Only top IT management really understands what the numbers represent – or, more accurately, are supposed to represent because, as we shall see further on, there is a significant margin of error. The rest, which means the vast majority of the IT department, have little idea of how their everyday work impacts the company's financial statements. They probably also don't particularly care, not because they're unprofessional, but because they don't see it as part of their responsibilities. They are there to do analysis, development, support or whatever; the finances are seen as the responsibility of their managers – or that of the finance department.

And yet, it is the everyday work of these very people, built on complex interrelationships between specialist teams, which drives the numbers. How can people who feel that IT financials are not part of their responsibilities provide accurate information which will ultimately be converted into financials to the tune of 2% to 8% of revenue and up to 50% of capital spend?

The answer, of course, is they can't. For example, a PSB Research poll in May 2009 of senior IT decision-makers found that as many as three quarters of them estimate a margin of error of 5-20% in their actual costs, while only 12% estimate a margin of error of less than 5%.[1] For a $100m IT budget, that means that the numbers could be out by $5-20m for three out of every four companies polled. In other words, it could be $80m as it could be $120m – which is not exactly small change.

The poll simply confirms what most of us suspect anyway. Over my many years in the industry, in both IT departments and at software vendors, I have regularly heard people – including senior managers – openly admit that they don't know the difference between capital expenditure (capex) and operating expense (opex)! These very same people then raise purchase orders (POs) in which the wrong choice of account could turn a $100,000 capital purchase into a current-year expense. Or they approve time entry based mainly on the number of hours their people work, instead of also verifying the underlying activities that drive capex and opex.

All of this wouldn't be that bad if the IT controllers from the finance department played the role of guardian and protector, and were able to catch such errors. Unfortunately, this is not always the case. Many companies suffer from the classic dilemma of IT people not knowing enough about finance, and finance people not knowing enough about IT. So IT gives the numbers to Finance, who often has to take most of it at face value. This is as true for budgets as it is for actuals. These same numbers are then sometimes charged back to the Business Units (BUs), who might have little idea of what they're paying for, and in turn have to take them at face value.

Software vendors that target IT departments usually don't fare much better. It is a truism in the software industry that vendors first latch on to a particular buzzword or market segment, and only then see about bringing their products and people up to speed. Apart from those with a very specific financial slant – eg, asset management, billing/chargeback and performance management vendors – the rest are probably as financially challenged as the IT departments they pitch to. While significant progress has been made in their products to cover more financial requirements, their people in sales, pre-sales and professional services are mainly project- and service-management focused, and are generally uncomfortable when discussions about portfolio management, cost management and chargebacks go below the waterline.

With ITFM (IT Financial Management) poised to become a new buzzword from 2010 onwards – see the Forrester report entitled "Market Overview: IT Financial Management Software" ("Further reading", Appendix 2) – this training gap will have to be addressed sooner or later for software vendors.

This led me to the idea of raising the financial awareness across the board at IT departments and at software vendors that sell to them. The result is this book, *"An Introduction to IT Project Financials – Budgeting, Cost Management and Chargebacks"*.

What this book is

This book explains the fundamentals of IT financials to professionals whose day jobs are primarily about technology and business processes, but whose everyday activities nonetheless have a huge impact on IT costs. The main focus is on software development projects because this is where business expectations are greatest and the financials most complex.

Poor IT financial practices result in a frustratingly high amount of non-value added tracking and reporting, and leave staff, projects and applications exposed to cost-cutting by default. Raising people's financial awareness would therefore result in the following key benefits:

- For the CIO: more timely and more accurate cost management.

- For business customers: more transparency in chargebacks and the chance to start focusing more on IT value than IT costs.

- For the finance department: a higher level of confidence in project budgets and IT financial reporting.

- For the rest of the IT department – or what's in it for me?

  o   significantly reduced administration time

  o   a better working environment in terms of staffing and funding.

What this book is not

This is not a detailed book, but simply an introduction, as the title makes clear. For readers looking for more extensive coverage of certain topics, there are numerous articles and books (see "Further reading" in Appendix 2).

It will no doubt come as a great relief to most readers that this is *not* a book about accounting – at least not directly. While certain accounting concepts are, of course, fundamental to any book on financials – eg, accruals and depreciation – we will only interest ourselves in their purpose and how they work from a practical perspective. We won't be bothered with the accounting entries they generate. So there'll be no talk of double-entry bookkeeping, journal entries, subsidiary ledgers or contra accounts (sigh of relief …). Even the words debit and credit are not used in this book – except to say that, to your credit, you are reading this book.

Finally, this book is not a platform for promoting best-practice methodologies such as CoBIT, ITIL or PMBOK, for example, which directly or indirectly cover IT financials. In their current versions, none of these methodologies do a particularly good job at this. But there are signs that this is beginning to change as IT financial management slowly becomes mainstream.

Who this book is for

This book is for all those constituents – from "grunts to execs" – with a vested interest in having an IT department with accurate and timely cost management, reduced administration time and more stable staffing and funding:

- The *whole* IT department, and not just the CIO and senior IT management.

- IT controllers from Finance, so that they can play a more active part in challenging the numbers they are presented with, instead of often having to take things at face value.

- Pre-sales and services consultants at software vendors that sell project- and service-related solutions to IT departments.

Qualifiers

- *IT Departments*: the scope of IT departments covered in this book is that of a general internal service provider, or a shared services organization, providing products and services to the rest of the business. We shall not be concerned in this book with the IT departments of consulting companies or software vendors that provide IT services to external clients.

- *Projects*: the term project as used in this book covers mainly business-software projects based on in-house development or the customization of enterprise software packages (both on-premises and hosted Software as a Service, or Saas). Technical projects concerning hardware and network infrastructure are only mentioned in passing, as they are usually few in number and don't present many challenges on the financial front.

- *IT vs IS*: Though some organizations distinguish between IT (Information Technology, or the operations group that manages the infrastructure and "keeps the lights on") and IS (Information Systems, or the development groups in contact with the business and responsible for projects), such a distinction would be overkill for this book. We therefore use the general term IT to refer to the entire IT department. This happens to correspond to how the rest of the business views the IT department anyway.

Reader feedback

In an internet age, writing is fortunately no longer a one-way street. So please feel free to visit my website at www.itfprojectfinancials.com, where you can provide feedback and even take part in short surveys on various topics.

1. For this study, PSB Research conducted 200 internet surveys of senior IT decision-makers in North America (US and Canada), Western Europe (UK, France and Germany), Asia Pacific (Australia, Japan, China, Singapore and India), Latin America (Brazil and Mexico), Eastern Europe (Russia) and the Middle East (United Arab Emirates).

Acknowledgements

If any of the readers of my previous books were to compare the Acknowledgements sections, they'd probably start experiencing a sense of déjà vu. And they'd be absolutely right! The subject of the book might change, but the role others play in helping to shape it is always the same.

As any author knows, you can't successfully bring a book to market without the help of others. It's one thing having a great idea and producing a draft manuscript from it, but it's quite another thing altogether turning it into a finished product. The 80/20 rule applies to writing too: 80% of the total effort is required to produce the first draft of a manuscript – inevitably replete with inaccuracies, inconsistencies and bad grammar – and the remaining 20% is necessary to turn it into something that people will actually read.

I would therefore once again like to pay a sincere tribute to all those people who had the unenviable task of finding time in their already-busy schedules to critically read through all or part of the manuscript. Not only did they manage to highlight inconsistencies and areas of disagreement, but they also helped to round off some of the rough edges of my writing style.

So many thanks to (in alphabetical order):

- Antonio Anastasi, Senior CRM Consultant, whose critical reading of the final formatted manuscript uncovered errors which had somehow fallen through the cracks. Antonio also provided valuable suggestions for the next edition of the book.

- Fouad Rwayane, Senior Consultant – IT Governance, at Compuware, whose combination of pre-sales and professional services experience around budgeting and cost management enabled valuable fine-tuning of certain key topics.

- Harry Ringwood, Senior Programme Manager – Consumer Health Care, at Merck Serono, whose ability to successfully straddle both finance and IT helped to firm up many of the financial elements in this book.

- Mark Pathmarajah, Managing Director of SwissPMO, whose sharp eye, combined with his three-way experience in financials, IT and business, helped to spot and correct potential generalizations. Mark also enabled me to better position the book from a target audience perspective.

- Regis Morizur, Programme Manager at Amadeus, whose in-the-trenches experience managing programme budgets played right to the themes of this book. Regis also provided valuable formatting recommendations which helped to structure the book in a more readable way.

- Robert Gentle, my twin brother and fellow-author, who, as always, probably had the worst task of all in that he had to review the "beta release" that preceded the first draft. Besides his usual corrections of my bad grammar, Robert also helped me to lighten the tone of a normally serious subject.

- Stefan Maron, Information Manager – Tech Ops, Marketing and Commercial, at Merck Serono, who managed to do the review during an intercontinental flight when he should have been relaxing from his hectic schedule. Stefan's broad experience in consulting and in managing complex budget situations helped to identify certain areas that needed some rework for a wider audience.

- Steve Beaumont, Lead Solution Consultant EMEA, at Apptio, and former EMEA Pre-sales Lead – IT Financial Management, at HP, whose keen insight from both his current and previous roles were right in the sweet spot of this book.

- Steve Woess, PMO Senior Manager at Business & Decision, whose strong experience in managing PMO financials, as well as in IT auditing, enabled me to understand much better the subtleties behind certain financial terms. Steve also helped to reposition the book from a market and title perspective.

- Thierry Baldantoni, PPM Subject Matter Expert, at Compuware, whose combined experience in sales support and professional services helped me to identify certain missing topics, which I subsequently included, resulting in a more balanced book.

Finally, this book would never have seen the light of day without the support of my wife and children, who accepted once again the family and career constraints that are required for me to get away with this strange hobby of mine of writing books every few years.

List of Abbreviations

ABC	Activity-Based Costing
APM	Application Portfolio Management
B-to-B	Business-to-Business
BU	Business Unit
Capex	Capital expenditure
CEO	Chief Executive Officer
CFO	Chief Financial Officer
CIO	Chief Information Officer
CoBIT	Control Objectives for Information and Related Technology
CRM	Customer Relationship Management
EBITDA	Earnings Before Interest, Taxes, Depreciation and Amortization
ERP	Enterprise Resource Planning
ESP	External Service Provider
ETC	Estimate to Complete
EUR	Euros
FY	Financial Year
GBP	British Pounds
GAAP	Generally Accepted Accounting Principles
GAS	General Accounting System
HR	Human Resources
IaaS	Infrastructure as a Service
IFRS	International Financial Reporting Standards

IRR	Internal Rate of Return
IS	Information Systems
IT	Information Technology
ITFM	IT Financial Management
ITIL	IT Infrastructure Library
MAS	Management Accounting System
NPV	Net Present Value
Opex	Operating expense
PaaS	Platform as a Service
PO	Purchase Order
PPM	Project Portfolio Management
PSA	Professional Services Automation
P&L	Profit and Loss
ROI	Return on Investment
R&D	Research and Development
SaaS	Software as a Service
SDLC	Software Development Life Cycle
SFA	Sales Force Automation
SLA	Service Level Agreement
TCO	Total Cost of Ownership
T&E	Travel and Entertainment
USD	US Dollars
YTD	Year-to-Date

Chapter 1

Why Bother? Or How Financials Affect Everyone in IT

"A million here, a million there, and soon you're talking about real money." (Everett Dirksen)

All financial terms introduced in this chapter are in *italics* and are explained in the "Glossary of Common Financial Terms" in Appendix 1. However, I recommend you first read this chapter in its entirety *before* going to the glossary. This will enable you to get a general idea of your level of financial awareness.

IT financials – the big picture

If you work in the IT department of a $1bn company (of which there are many – the smallest Fortune 1000 company has sales of $1.7bn), then:

- Your IT *budget* is anywhere from $20-80m (2-8% of revenue).

- IT spending represents up to 50% of *capital expenditure*, which is what the company invests in *assets* like plant, property and equipment.

- About 20% of the IT budget is for new things – ie, projects, and the remaining 80% is for running and maintaining production applications, or keeping the lights on (Gartner, Forrester). See Fig. 1.1.

- The lifetime costs of an IT application are on average 5 times the initial project investment, which explains the 80/20 ratio above.

These financial realities have far-reaching consequences in terms of IT budgeting, cost management and how IT is generally viewed in the enterprise.

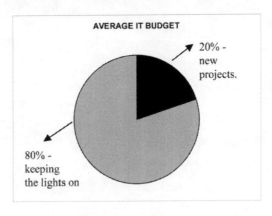

Figure 1.1 Sample IT budget

How IT financials affect everyone

If you think that IT financials are just for the bean counters, think again! Consider the following only-too-real situation.

During the annual fire drill when the CFO requires another round of budget cuts for the current financial year, which department do you think is likely to contribute the lion's share: R&D, manufacturing, sales, marketing, customer service? Probably none of these. How about IT? Bingo! The department that is usually viewed as a bunch of techies who know how to spend money but usually don't deliver on time and on budget, is usually the biggest contributor.

So how does the CIO come up with a shortlist of what to cut? Let's consider two scenarios.

Scenario 1: financial fire-fighting

Scenario 1 starts with an urgent e-mail to all project managers and application managers for their latest numbers, ie *actuals* and *forecast*. Instead of calmly getting the information out of a Project Portfolio Management (PPM) - or Service Management (SM) tool, there is usually a frantic scramble for information and updating of spreadsheets. This is especially true for software development projects which, by definition, are moving targets compared to the relative stability of production applications. A hasty check is done on how far back in time the most reliable Year-to-Date (YTD) actuals are, and a guesstimate is done for the forecast. This is made all the more difficult by late invoicing – not always reflected in *commitments*, or alternatively in *accruals* – and late payments by the Accounts Payable department, which is still struggling with the new Enterprise Resource Planning (ERP) system. And you still haven't got around to checking that the new temp is correctly doing the *receiving* so that the Customer Relationship Management (CRM) integrator's milestone payments – which represents the lion's share of your budget – are booked to the correct *capex* or *opex* accounts,. As for the work done by other departments on your project, from software license purchases and setup to infrastructure support, you've got little visibility on the status of their Purchase Orders *(POs)*, the accuracy of their people's *time entry* and what will be booked to capex and to opex.

You can probably guess the accuracy and reliability of the numbers finally presented 24 hours later – remember the survey mentioned in the Introduction, which found out that 3 out of 4 respondents estimated a margin of error of 5-20% in their costs.

Based on this information, some projects might be cancelled, others put on hold, that long-awaited application upgrade will be postponed to next year, that performance-monitoring tool that you were about to purchase is not going to materialize, that DBA post you were just about to fill will be frozen – well, you get the picture. In summary, important decisions will be made which affect everyone, from the most junior software developer to the most senior programme director.

And you thought that financials were just for senior management and for IT controllers in Finance!

Scenario 2: IT financials under control

In scenario 2, you are a project manager and still have to provide your latest numbers for the cost-cutting exercise, but unlike your peers, you manage your costs very well. You know that if you don't do this, your project and your team's destiny will mostly be under other people's control. You have a realistic budget which catches all categories of costs, ensuring nothing falls through the cracks. The corresponding actuals are then accurately captured and correctly booked to capex or opex. You are not impacted much by late invoicing and late payments to your vendors because your commitments and accruals correctly reflect uninvoiced work. You ensure your staff enter their time on a weekly basis because you know that anything later than that would compromise the accuracy of your people costs. You closely monitor the work of other departments which support your project, because you know that the resulting financials are not their main concern.

Finally, at the start of each month, you collate all of this information and sit down with your team leads to update the forecast, which is all the more accurate because of a sense of ownership of the overall numbers, not just by your key people, but also by the rest of the team. Everyone understands how their actions can positively or negatively impact the project's financials – and hence their own jobs. Monthly variations of planned vs actuals, which you monitor, average about +/-10%, and are quite easy to explain because of the cost transparency.

So when the CIO draws up his shortlist for the cost-cutting exercise, your project escapes relatively unscathed. If you do have to give a little, the effect would be limited because you are clearly able to identify which areas would be affected and be able to adjust your scope and schedule so as not to impact overall quality. But the CIO has little reason to single out your project unjustly – after all, your monthly variations of planned vs actuals are pretty accurate, so there is little reason for him to question the accuracy of your forecast for the rest of the year. And since you even do a 12-month rolling forecast, your visibility stretches right into the next financial year.

Now clearly, we'd all like to be in this second scenario, wouldn't we? Yet I can bet you a thousand dollars – which you could probably easily pay out of the margin of error in last month's project reporting – that you're probably more familiar with the first scenario.

Even without cost-cutting, this second scenario would still represent good project financial management. In fact, it should be par for the course. Unfortunately, it isn't. To make it so would require the following pre-requisites, all of which will be covered in this book:

- Raising the general financial awareness of all IT staff – and not just senior management – because ultimately, it is everyone's actions which contribute to the accuracy and timeliness of the overall numbers.

- Implementing basic financial processes for budgeting and cost management within a project management framework that goes beyond just project delivery.

- Implementing the appropriate PPM and related financial tools to support these processes.

The three main IT financials processes

1 - *Planning and Budgeting*

The strategic business plan defines a company's long-term goals (usually 5-10 years) with respect to its target market and the roadmap needed to achieve them. This is then broken down into a short/medium-term planning horizon (usually 1-3 years) during which certain things need to be done, resulting in a marketing plan, an operations plan, an R&D plan, etc.

When IT is a strategic part of the business, there is also an IT plan; otherwise the IT plan would be part of the overall financial plan. In either case, there would be medium/long-term IT goals, ranging from centralized operations and infrastructure (eg, following a merger or acquisition) to providing customers with 24/7 access to information (eg, for competitive differentiation). This would give rise to "big-ticket" projects like enterprise-wide ERP or CRM, which can run for 1-3 years.

The three main IT financials processes are shown in Fig. 1.2.

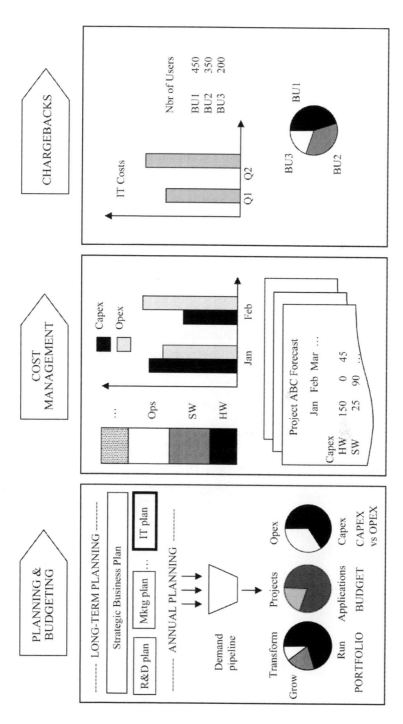

Figure 1.2 The three main IT-financials processes

Then there are shorter-term projects needed to meet current- or next-year business objectives, eg a new data warehouse or a technical infrastructure upgrade. These are usually defined as part of the annual planning cycle.

Finally, there are production applications to run and maintain, which is what projects become once they have been delivered. This activity continues throughout the 5-8 year useful life of the software asset.

In summary, the IT plan is the basis for delivering products and services comprising:

- Projects, both medium/long-term with a planning horizon of 1-3 years, and short-term with a planning horizon of 1 year or less. Projects represent approximately 20% of the IT budget.

- Running and maintaining production applications, which represent approximately 80% of the IT budget.

The upshot of all this is that IT is simply one more part of the company – together with Marketing, R&D, etc – asking for money to spend as part of their operating plans. This process takes place during the annual budget-planning or investment-planning exercise, a combination of top-down and bottom-up budgeting during which departments specify what they plan to spend in order to do their job. Some of this spending will be capex (eg software licenses and development costs), which will be *depreciated* in subsequent years, and some will be opex (eg annual maintenance and data-migration costs), which will hit the *P&L* during the current year.

Depending on the financial maturity of the company, budget planning or investment planning can be part of an objective *portfolio management* approach. More often than not, though, it is part of a simple project prioritization approach based on a combination of business objectives, more or less subjective business cases and – good old-fashioned business-sponsor influence.

2 - Cost Management

Once the final operating plans have been approved, cost management and forecasting assume critical importance:

- Cost management, to track actual costs incurred, ensure they are correctly booked to capex vs opex, and to explain any deviations from the plan.

- Forecasting (or ongoing budgeting), to adjust the spending with respect to the original budget based on actual costs incurred and projected costs remaining.

Actual costs are booked into the *general accounting system,* whereas forecasting is recorded in the *management accounting system.*

3 - Chargebacks

Finally, once the corresponding products and services have been delivered according to the IT plan, the costs are either centralized as part of a corporate cost centre (ie, IT is "free" for the various BUs, since they don't pay for it directly) or charged back in the form of *allocations* and *cross-charges* (ie, the BUs pay directly for IT, whose costs figure on their P&Ls).

Companies charge back IT costs either for financial reasons (eg, for cost recovery or because of corporate policies which require all costs to be transferred to BUs) or as a lever to help balance supply and demand (by eliminating the "free-lunch" syndrome whereby buyers will naturally tend to ask for more when they are not the final payers).

Your personal financial reality check

How much of what you read in this chapter was new to you? Were you generally aware of the IT-financials big picture outlined at the start of this chapter? Did you know how the IT plan fits into the overall strategic business plan, and where the annual IT budget comes from? How comfortable were you with the terms used in this chapter, like capex, opex, budget, forecast, actuals, accruals, commitments, depreciation and P&Ls?

If your answers are mainly in the negative, then go straight to the "Glossary of Common Financial Terms" in Appendix 1, which has a suggested reading sequence for the financially challenged.

If your answers are mainly in the positive, then advance to Go and collect $200 (in opex).

Chapter 2

Planning and Budgeting

"The budgeting process at most companies has to be the most ineffective practice in management. It sucks the energy, time, fun and big dreams out of an organization." (Jack Welch)

Demand management

Demand for IT products and services originates from customers in the BUs in the form of ideas or opportunities, with high-level information on timing, costs and benefits.

At the one extreme, IT is simply an internal service provider operating under a traditional client/vendor model and focused on satisfying user requirements. It is in a sense a passive order-taker disconnected from the business and not really involved in understanding what lies behind customer demand.

At the other extreme, IT is a strategic differentiator and is part of a joint IT/business group responsible for process improvement and business innovation. Here we would have account managers responsible for understanding customer demand and full IT participation in the decision-making and approval process.

There are two categories of demand – planned and unplanned:

- Planned demand arises as part of the annual budget planning or investment planning process (covered in the next section), which results in the IT Plan and the corresponding budget for the next financial year. Planned demand comprises projects and keeping the lights on.

- Unplanned demand corresponds to the huge amount of unpredictable work that IT does which is not contained in well-defined project- and application structures. These include things like change requests, feature requests and bug fixes, which arise, for example, from changing business and regulatory environments, changes in strategy, company reorganizations, mergers and acquisitions and insufficiently tested systems. Some of these requests will become input for the next planning cycle, but most will have to be fulfilled inside of the current budget cycle.

For those who believe in the myth of the sacrosanct annual IT Plan, remember, it's just that – a myth. In the real world demand is coming in every single day, so the challenge is to capture that demand, both planned and unplanned, as early as possible, expose the high-level business justification and set up an ongoing dialogue between IT and its customers. This enables the management of a demand pipeline (see Fig. 2.1).

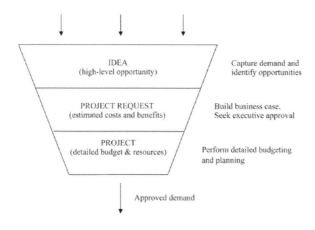

Figure 2.1 Managing demand

An opportunity analysis on this pipeline, based on an appropriate scoring model, will give rise to an initial screening and validation process, which will enable an idea to move down to the next stage and become a project request. Typical examples of filtering criteria for a scoring model are expected revenue increase, expected cost reduction, regulatory compliance or operational improvements.

Project requests are then further qualified in order to build a business case, which will be based on a combination of business alignment, costs, benefits, technology alignment, risk and IT resource and scheduling constraints.

Finally, once the business case has been approved, the project request moves down to the stage where it becomes a project – though strictly speaking these would not just be new projects, but also key enhancements and upgrades to production applications. At this stage detailed planning and budgeting takes place. Note that though the project is approved (as in "this is a good idea and we should be doing it") it will only exit the funnel for execution if funding is available.

So what has demand management got to do with IT financials? Simply this: without a demand pipeline, the annual planning process essentially takes the form of a frantic organizational scramble over a 1-2 month period (the greater the sums involved, the less time you are given!) as people rush to put some numbers together so that they can "turn in their projects for next year" In such an environment, the chances are high that investment planning will follow a subjective project-by-project approach, rather than the more rational portfolio-based approach, which we shall now look at.

Portfolio-based investment planning

To nobody's surprise, IT demand exceeds supply; the business ends up asking for more products and services than the IT department is able to deliver based on resource and capacity constraints – and indeed based on the ability of the business to fund it all. With so much competing demand coming into the pipeline, and only so much being approved at the other end, it would make sense to spread it across a number of well-defined investment categories based on a combination of business objectives, expected return and risk.

An analogy is a personal-investment portfolio, which would comprise, for example, cash, stocks, bonds and a mortgage, each of which represents a different mix of risk and return (see Fig. 2.2).

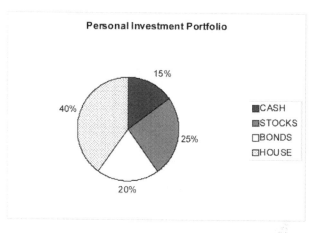

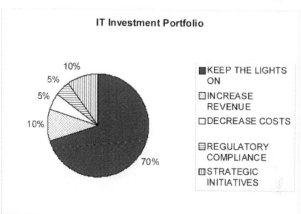

Figure 2.2 Portfolio examples

When applied to project investments, portfolio management is called Project Portfolio Management (PPM). But because projects only represent about 20% of IT costs, it makes sense to also include the remaining 80%, which represents applications. The combined approach would simply be called IT Portfolio Management.

An IT portfolio should be well-balanced across new projects and running production systems, with investment criteria based on business objectives, expected return and risk. It should also be managed over time to ensure it continues to meet business objectives, with the category mix varying based on changing business requirements like acquisitions, competitive threats or regulatory compliance. For example, a serious downturn in a company's market sector might result in it reducing the funding for everything except keeping the lights on, just as an upturn in the market might lead it to increasing funding on strategic innovations.

A basic example of investment categories that can be used for IT portfolio management is:

- Keeping the lights on

- Generating revenue

- Reducing costs

- Regulatory compliance

- Strategic initiatives

By scoring all demand against an appropriate portfolio mix (eg, 70% keeping the lights on, 10% generating revenue, 5% reducing costs, 10% ensuring regulatory compliance and 5% launching strategic initiatives), a company is better able to select and manage its IT investments so that limited resources are assigned to achievable, business-aligned goals. This would be done in the project-request stage as part of the approval process in conjunction with the business case.

Portfolio planning also allows a company to launch projects and fund applications that might otherwise stand little chance of being approved based solely on the business case. For example, an experimental, high-risk project might not be approved if viewed in isolation, nor might it receive ongoing funding once it went into production as an application. However, when viewed from a portfolio perspective, it might be approved as say, part of the "Strategic Initiatives" category.

Portfolio planning would not only look at demand to see whether it corresponds to business objectives – it would also take the reverse approach and look at the business objectives to see whether there are too few or too many corresponding project requests. For example, an analysis of the sample project-investment portfolio of Fig. 2.3 might reveal that the business objective "decrease costs" has too much funding, whereas the arguably more important objective of "increase revenue" has too few projects. After all, no company ever saved its way to prosperity. This might result in a decision to modify the portfolio mix to obtain a more balanced portfolio in terms of investment objectives.

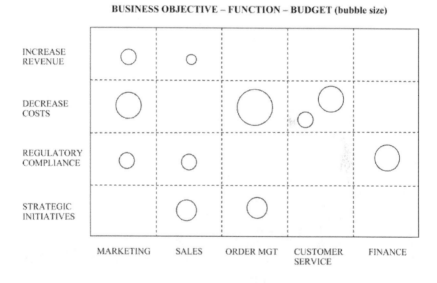

Figure 2.3 Sample investment portfolio breakdown by function

Finally, portfolio planning doesn't end with prioritization and approval. Once the corresponding projects have been launched and are under way, we then have to monitor the performance of the portfolio over time to ensure it is still meeting our initial objectives.

The alternative to a portfolio-based approach is a project-by-project approach – unfortunately the norm in most companies – in which projects are approved as a collection of individual and often unrelated items. This lack of categorization makes it difficult to invest rationally. It also makes it difficult to react to a changing business environment. So instead of adjusting spend based on investment category criteria, we end up doing so based on individual project criteria (suitably biased by business-sponsor influence ...). Investment on a project-by-project basis would be the equivalent of financial investment based on individual financial instruments – eg, company A, bond B and currency C. Taken individually, such investments might make sense, but taken collectively, they could leave you with a poorly-performing portfolio – and an inability to know which items to adjust when the market changes.

Building the IT plan and budget

So how do we define the IT budget? What gets in (besides the CEO's pet project...), what stays out and what gets parked for later?

The IT budget would basically be prepared in three stages: wish list, approved work and funded work. The wish list would be the total pipeline at budget preparation time, which would be the sum of all ideas, project requests and projects. Note again the importance of demand management: without a demand pipeline to feed the budget process, ideas and project requests would have to be quickly thrown together in the space of a month. Needless to say, such a rush job would be neither accurate nor objective.

A filtering and screening process would then reduce this wish list to an approved list, suitably categorized into portfolios as explained above. This would represent things the company must do (like keeping the lights on and regulatory projects) and would like to do (all other project requests and projects). Finally, based on available funding, the approved work is reduced to funded work which will actually be done. This becomes the annual IT plan and budget.

The two main methods of budgeting

The overall IT budget which results from the annual investment planning process explained above is a combination of top-down and bottom-up budgeting, depending on the information available at the time and the budgeting methods used.

There are two main forms of budgeting:

- *Baseline or incremental budgeting*: when operations are fairly predictable and repeatable, the logical approach is to use the previous year's budget, with an adjustment based on actuals, inflation and expected events during the coming year. This is baseline budgeting, which has the advantage of speed, simplicity and generally high accuracy, since it is based on real-world historical data. The disadvantage is that it does not encourage people to question previous assumptions or to consider new ways of working, which could result in a lower budget.

- *Zero-based budgeting*: for non-repeatable activities like projects, budgeting has to start from scratch, hence the term zero-based budgeting. The obvious advantage of this approach is that it encourages a more disciplined analysis and justification of all costs. The downside is the time, effort and complexity required. The unfortunate reality in most IT departments is that project managers simply don't have the time for budgeting, which therefore becomes a rush job (their day jobs don't miraculously adjust to make time for the annual planning process ...). Not only that, few have the financial background or training to do so properly – part of the very premise of this book. And finally, any errors or omissions might not be caught by IT financial controllers, since they don't always have the background to question the numbers. So the quality of zero-based budgeting can vary significantly based on the people doing it, and on the level of oversight provided by Finance.

In the real world, IT budgeting is usually a combination of baseline budgeting and zero-based budgeting.

The main categories of IT costs

Let us review the activities behind IT projects and applications and summarize the various cost components.

A project is delivered by a software development team (from an IT department or an External Service Provider or ESP) that designs, develops (in-house development), configures (off-the-shelf software package) and implements the first release or version. The resulting applications physically reside on infrastructure (hardware, system software and networks) and are run and supported by an operations or production team. Subsequent releases or upgrades (also called maintenance) are then brought out at regular intervals to meet new or changing business requirements, usually by the same development team that produced the first release, and are then put into production to replace the previous one. This cycle continues up to the end of the useful life of the application, which can be anywhere from 5 to 10 years.

Some companies take applications one level higher and map them to IT services (ideally part of a service catalogue, complete with pricing), for example, providing e-mail service, a laptop and a mobile phone to a new hire. IT departments can also provide services to each other. For example, a project manager can request infrastructure and network services from the Infrastructure Department in order to meet her deliverables. In general, a service is something with clearly defined costs and delivery criteria (hence the term SLA or Service Level Agreement). You could buy it from an ESP, or outsource it to a vendor that is able to do it more cost-effectively.

Most business applications, though, are not really services but simply an enabling environment which IT provides for getting something done. For example, an SFA (Sales Force Automation) application enables the sales force to be more effective; a data warehouse enables sales and marketing operations to do analysis of sales versus market share.

Projects, applications and services result in the following cost categories, which form the basis of IT budgeting:

- Hardware (essentially IT equipment, from servers to network hubs)

- Software (application and system software)

- People (internal staff, contractors and consultants working on activities ranging from design and development to data migration and operations)

- External services (telecoms, disaster recovery, outsourcing ...)

- Travel and Entertainment (T&E)

Not included in the above would be employee benefits, plus general IT overhead such as facilities, recruiting, training, analysis of emerging technologies, internal cross-charging from other departments (HR, Finance...), management and reporting. Adding all of this to the above cost categories yields the so-called fully-loaded costs, and it is these that should ideally be used for budgeting so as to get the full cost picture. All reference to internal staff costs from here onwards refers to fully-loaded costs.

The main categories of IT costs are summarized in Fig. 2.4.

Figure 2.4 The main IT cost categories

Budgeting rules for capex vs opex

Money comes in various colours, from green in the US to all the colours of the rainbow in other countries. In IT, money comes in only two colours – capex and opex.

Which categories of IT costs should be capitalized?

Which of them should be expensed? The answers can be found in various national and international regulations and accounting standards which lay down clear guidelines for capex vs opex when developing software for internal use.

So what do these accounting rules cover? Mainly the following three phases in software development:

- Preliminary project stage or evaluation phase, which establishes the technical feasibility of the project. This is charged to opex, because if the project ended here, there would be no asset to speak of.

- Software development or application configuration phase. This is capex, because the end result is an asset, comprising software (bought or built), hardware and infrastructure.

- Post implementation or production phase. This is opex, because these are day-to-day running costs. Note that software license maintenance is opex, whereas the licenses themselves (previous point) are capex.

Now if only it were that simple! Unfortunately, IT is not science or engineering (even though we often like to think it is). For example:

- Functional design is opex and technical design is capex, but the border between the two is often blurred, especially when done by collaborative teams.

- The financial guidelines assume a strict Software Development Life Cycle (SDLC) waterfall methodology, so applying it to Agile with its collaborative approach and short cycles would result in less capitalization – even though over time, you could have an equally, if not more, cost-effective asset.

- When in production, upgrades or enhancements are capitalizable, whereas small changes and maintenance are not, even though they both have development costs.

- The development costs of a one-time data-migration interface are not capitalizable because it does not result in a long-term asset.

- T&E are normally expenses – except when they are part of a capitalizable activity!

In short, there is room for interpretation, resulting in differences in the way companies capitalize IT costs. So how does the average project manager or application owner – for whom most of the above is probably news – ensure that her budget complies with accounting rules and can stand up to an audit? The answer lies in her level of financial awareness, the support she gets from the finance department and the degree to which ERP systems can be set up to automatically implement some of these rules.

Financial support for budgeting

In personal life, you can sometimes get away with saying "my wife handles the financials". In IT unfortunately, you often have to handle your own financials, for which you will need support.

There are varying levels of support provided by Finance to IT during the budgeting process. At one end of the spectrum, project managers and application managers need only provide the monetary totals, and the capex vs opex breakdown is handled by financial analysts or IT controllers. At the other end, financial support is minimal, and IT budget owners are supposed to provide not just the monetary totals for each cost category, but also their capex-vs-opex breakdown. I have seen both extremes, and it should come as no surprise to learn that when IT project managers and application managers with low financial awareness put together capex and opex budgets, the end result in terms of budget accuracy and financial compliance can only be questionable.

Some companies have internal processes around IT budgeting which require that all budgets be submitted to a budget review board whose role it is to challenge the numbers. Project managers and application managers have to then defend their budgets and demonstrate that they are in line with IT budgeting rules (eg, run through all cost categories to ensure nothing has been left out – by accident or design) and comply with capex-vs-opex guidelines.

A sample project budget

Surprisingly, for something as elementary as an IT budget, there are numerous versions and templates floating around on the web, varying from high-level cost categories to detailed task-level costs that can even be part of a project plan. There is therefore no right or wrong budget format, only the one that allows you to manage to the level of detail you require.

For this chapter we have chosen something intermediate which goes down to at least one level of detail and reflects the phase of the project, thus enabling a capex-vs-opex breakdown.

| | | | LOCAL CCY | | REPORTING CCY | | | | Assessment | |
| | | | | | | | | | JAN | |
CATEGORY	ITEM	QTY	UNIT COST (x1000)	CCY	UNIT COST kEUR	COST TYPE	% CAP	% OP	Cap	Op
Hardware	Infrastructure usage	1	90.0	EUR	90.0	One-off	0%	100%	0.0	0.0
	Laptops for testing	3	1.5	USD	3.5	One-off	0%	100%	0.0	0.0
									0.0	*0.0*
Software	CRM software - licenses	50	1.0	EUR	50.0	One-off	100%	0%	50.0	0.0
	CRM software - maintenance	1	10.0	EUR	10.0	One-off	0%	100%	0.0	10.0
									50.0	*10.0*
Integrator	Assessment and requirements	1	40.0	USD	30.8	One-off	0%	100%	0.0	30.8
	Milestone 1 - Design	1	150.0	USD	115.4	Milestone	50%	50%		
	Milestone 2 - Dev and testing	1	250.0	USD	192.3	Milestone	100%	0%		
	Milestone 3 - Deployment	1	100.0	USD	76.9	Milestone	0%	100%		
									0.0	*30.8*
Internal staff	Project Manager (UK)	1	10.0	GBP	8.3	Month	0%	100%	0.0	8.3
	Business Analyst (FR)	1	8.0	EUR	8.0	Month	0%	100%	0.0	8.0
	Business Analyst (US)	1	10.0	USD	7.7	Month	100%	0%	7.7	0.0
									7.7	*16.3*
Contractors	Tech specialist (US)	1	16.0	USD	12.3	Month	100%	0%	0.0	0.0
	Data specialist (UK)	1	15.0	GBP	12.5	Month	0%	100%		
									0.0	*0.0*
Consulting	Software consulting services	1	50.0	EUR	50.0	One-off	0%	100%	0.0	0.0
	Software technical services	1	20.0	EUR	20.0	Month	100%	0%		
									0.0	*0.0*
Travel	T&E - assessment	6	1.0	EUR	6.0	One-off	0%	100%	0.0	6.0
	T&E - testing	3	1.0	EUR	3.0	One-off	100%	0%		
									0.0	*6.0*
									7.7	53.1
									60.8	

Figure 2.5a Example of a budget for a CRM pilot project (continued on opposite page)

| | Design | | | | Development and Testing | | | | | | Deployment | | TOTAL | |
| ITEM | JAN | | FEB | | MAR | | APR | | MAY | | JUN | | | |
	Cap	Op	Cap	Op	Cap	Op	Cap	Op	Cap	Op	Cap	Op	Cap	Op
Infrastructure usage											0.0	90.0	0.0	90.0
Laptops for testing							0.0	3.5					0.0	3.5
	0.0	0.0	0.0	0.0	0.0	0.0	0.0	3.5	0.0	0.0	0.0	90.0	0.0	93.5
CRM software - licenses													50.0	0.0
CRM software - maintenance													0.0	10.0
													50.0	10.0
Assessment and requirements	0.0	30.8											0.0	30.8
Milestone 1 - Design					57.7	57.7							57.7	57.7
Milestone 2 - Dev and testing									192.3	0.0			192.3	0.0
Milestone 3 - Deployment											0.0	76.9	0.0	76.9
	0.0	30.8	0.0	0.0	57.7	57.7	0.0	0.0	192.3	0.0	0.0	76.9	250.0	165.4
Project Manager (UK)	0.0	8.3	0.0	8.3	0.0	8.3	0.0	8.3	0.0	8.3	0.0	8.3	0.0	50.0
Business Analyst (FR)	0.0	8.0	0.0	8.0					0.0	8.0			0.0	24.0
Business Analyst (US)	7.7	0.0	7.7	0.0					7.7	0.0			23.1	0.0
	7.7	16.3	7.7	16.3	0.0	8.3	0.0	8.3	7.7	16.3	0.0	8.3	23.1	74.0
Tech specialist (US)			12.3	0.0	12.3	0.0	12.3	0.0	12.3	0.0			49.2	0.0
Data specialist (UK)					0.0	12.5	0.0	12.5	0.0	12.5			0.0	37.5
			12.3	0.0	12.3	12.5	12.3	12.5	12.3	12.5			49.2	37.5
Software consulting services			0.0	50.0									0.0	50.0
Software technical services					20.0	0.0	20.0	0.0	20.0	0.0			60.0	0.0
			0.0	50.0	20.0	0.0	20.0	0.0	20.0	0.0			60.0	50.0
T&E - assessment	0.0	6.0											0.0	6.0
T&E - testing							3.0	0.0					3.0	0.0
	0.0	6.0					3.0	0.0					3.0	6.0
TOTAL	7.7	53.1	20.0	66.3	90.0	78.5	35.3	24.3	232.3	28.8	0.0	175.3	385.3	426.3
	60.8		86.3		168.5		59.6		261.1		175.3		811.7	

Assessment | Design | Development and Testing | Deployment

CATEGORY	JAN Cap	JAN Op	FEB Cap	FEB Op	MAR Cap	MAR Op	APR Cap	APR Op	MAY Cap	MAY Op	JUN Cap	JUN Op	TOTAL Cap	TOTAL Op
Hardware	0.0	0.0	0.0	0.0	0.0	0.0	0.0	3.5	0.0	0.0	0.0	90.0	0.0	93.5
Software	50.0	10.0	0.0	0.0	0.0	0.0	0.0	0.0	0.0	0.0	0.0	0.0	50.0	10.0
Integrator	0.0	30.8	0.0	0.0	57.7	57.7	0.0	0.0	192.3	0.0	0.0	76.9	250.0	165.4
Internal staff	7.7	16.3	7.7	16.3	0.0	8.3	0.0	8.3	7.7	16.3	0.0	8.3	23.1	74.0
Contractors	0.0	0.0	12.3	0.0	12.3	12.5	12.3	12.5	12.3	12.5	0.0	0.0	49.2	37.5
Consulting	0.0	0.0	0.0	50.0	20.0	0.0	20.0	0.0	20.0	0.0	0.0	0.0	60.0	50.0
Travel	0.0	6.0	0.0	0.0	0.0	0.0	3.0	0.0	0.0	0.0	0.0	0.0	3.0	6.0
	7.7	53.1	20.0	66.3	90.0	78.5	35.3	24.3	232.3	28.8	0.0	175.3	385.3	426.3
Run rate	60.8		86.3		168.5		59.6		261.1		175.3		811.7	

Figure 2.5b Roll-up of Fig 2.5a

Fig. 2.5a shows a sample budget – spread over two pages for reasons of size – for an international CRM pilot project. Some comments on this budget:

- The project is reported in euros, but costs can be incurred in local currency (euros, pounds or dollars – or EUR, GBP and USD in currency-speak). So items budgeted in local currency have to be converted to the reporting currency.

- The laptop purchases in this example are opex. Depending on country and company accounting rules, personal computers and laptops below a certain threshold – for example five thousand dollars – are considered as opex. Leased hardware can be capex or opex, depending on the type of lease.

- CRM software licenses are capex, but the associated annual maintenance is opex.

- The CRM integrator's milestone payments are capex or opex, depending on the project phase.

- Internal costs are fully-loaded.

- T&E are capex or opex, depending on the project phase.

Fig. 2.5b shows the budget rolled up to a summary level by cost category.

Budgeting for infrastructure

A budget should always include any infrastructure costs, both for the project phase and subsequently when in production. Well, "why wouldn't it?", you might ask. Simply because some companies manage their infrastructure budgets separately from the underlying projects and applications. They then allocate the costs out across multiple applications – or even the whole company. This makes sense when infrastructure is shared across multiple projects and applications, or is considered to form part of the "common good", like roads in a community. But if this is not the case, then the absence of infrastructure costs from a budget could unintentionally give the impression that projects and applications are cheaper than they actually are – thus biasing investment decisions. They might also increase the IT costs of other departments or BUs that have nothing to do with a particular project or application. Correctly allocating the usage costs of shared infrastructure is not always easy, but at the end of the day project and application budgets must include their fair share of infrastructure capital costs.

How budgeting drives resource and capacity planning

Besides its purely financial aspect, budgeting plays a key role in helping to determine how many resources are needed in IT for the next financial year. When project budgets are defined at the level of detail as shown in Fig. 2.5a, with effort suitably broken down by role over time, eg a Business Analyst for 3 months from February through April, a budget consolidation would yield a pretty accurate picture of project resource and capacity requirements for the coming year.

When combined with role-based effort estimates for ideas and project requests in the pipeline – see Fig. 2.1 – the overall result would yield a first cut of the resources and capacity that would be required for all of the demand in the organization.

Budget considerations for cloud computing

Like any self-respecting author writing on IT these days, I had to include at least one reference to cloud computing, for marketing reasons! But in this case, I think it's legitimate, so here we go.

Cloud computing is based on a monthly rental fee for external services hosted in a data centre – eg, per user for an application (Software as a Service, or Saas), by capacity for a server (Infrastructure as a Service, or IaaS), or by usage for a software development environment (Platform as a Service, or PaaS). There are no capital costs because there is no hardware purchased nor software assets created – except in the case of buy-and-host, in which you buy and configure your own software (capex), then turn it over to a vendor to host and run externally (opex). Apart from this, cloud computing is pure opex.

This can have significant implications for IT budgeting, for two reasons:

- Firstly, CIOs usually "prefer" capex to opex because, from an IT budget perspective, it pushes out today's costs to future years. This is explained in the Glossary in Appendix 1 when talking about capital costs.

- Secondly, you could argue from a Total-Cost-of-Ownership (TCO) perspective that the longer you keep a system, the more expensive rental becomes, since depreciation, unlike rental, has an end date after which the asset is considered paid.

There is an article which puts these questions into perspective called "Capex vs Opex: most people miss the point about cloud economics" (see "Further reading" in Appendix 2). I will simply summarize the highlights here:

- Monthly rental is usually predictable; you can therefore plan around it. When was the last time you heard about a predictable IT project budget?

- You can scale your user base up or down – or even pull out altogether – by opting in or out at any time as the business changes. For an in-house system, however, once your project is over and depreciation has started, you are committed to accounting for it right through to the end of its useful life of 3-5 years – whether you like it or not, and regardless of how your user base evolves. And if you want to pull out, you have to write off the asset against current-year earnings – resulting in a hit to the IT budget (see "Write off" in the Glossary in Appendix 1).

- For an apples-with-apples comparison, cloud computing vendors (serving multiple customers) should logically be able to do things more cost-effectively than an IT department (serving a single customer).

Of course, there are other factors which drive decisions around cloud computing, from data security to ease of integration. But when it comes to costs, it's not just about capex, opex and TCO, it's also about planning predictability and business flexibility.

Project budgets are just estimates – expect them to change

Yes, you read correctly! You might think this is heresy, but first read on.

Given the frequent cost overruns of IT projects, we

would ideally like to be able to define during the planning phase a detailed budget, so that the business case can be based on costs which are as accurate as possible. Unfortunately, this is wishful thinking, for a very fundamental reason: the detailed functional requirements (which are necessary to define what the technical solution will be) are not yet known at this stage. This is only to be expected, since it would take at least a few weeks to define these detailed requirements, and you wouldn't be able to do this until the project has been approved.

We consequently wouldn't be able to define an accurate budget anyway. In fact, in some cases we might not even know what the final solution will be in terms of technology or product (buy or build). Consequently, any budgeting will necessarily be an estimate. Even the sample budget of Fig. 2.5a is an estimate, as exceptionally detailed as it may be. Most project budgets during the planning phase are estimated at a higher level than this. Indeed, it is not uncommon to have some project budgets estimated to a round number with a 50/50 capex/opex split – and understandably so, since getting down to the level of detail of Fig. 2.5a requires lots of work and significant domain expertise in the solution space and the likely technological solution.

You will no doubt have noted the conundrum here. In order to define a detailed budget, you first need to define the detailed requirements (since that is what will enable you to define the technological solution and how much it will cost). However, in order to define the detailed requirements – as opposed to just high-level requirements – you need to mobilize people from both IT and the business for at least a couple of weeks. But you cannot do this until the project has been approved – based on a business case which requires the detailed budget and project schedule! We shall call this circularity "the commitment conundrum" – see Fig. 2.6.

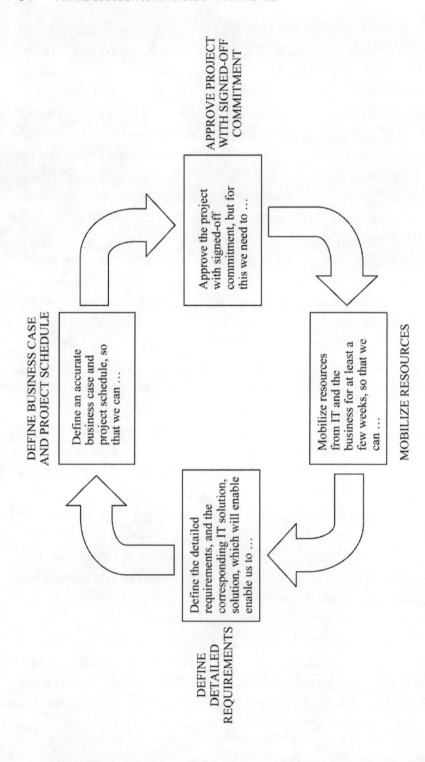

Figure 2.6 The commitment conundrum

The commitment conundrum leads us to a fundamental conclusion. During the investment planning phase, you can only define an estimated budget based on high-level requirements. This estimated budget will evolve once the project is validated and moves to the project-planning phase – and (yes, you guessed it!) will evolve yet again once the project is under way. Hence the importance of ongoing budgeting – or forecasting – which will be covered in the next chapter.

What this means is that you cannot define a budget that is cast in stone, and which you can later hold an IT department or an ESP responsible for delivering against contractually – despite the theory that says that you can.

Unfortunately, most companies view their IT departments as building contractors that are supposed to deliver on time, budget and spec (even though the specs are hardly ever defined at budget-definition time). And the IT departments themselves then contribute to this misconception by defining project success criteria mainly in terms of on-time and on-budget delivery!

At the end of the day, from a financials perspective, all IT project budgets are just estimates (application budgets for keeping the lights on are more predictable and therefore more reliable). The CFO and the finance department should therefore expect these to evolve later in the year (the CIO, of course, knows they will!). As such, Finance should not only focus on helping IT to build the budget during the annual planning phase, but also provide active support during the rest of the year for cost management and forecasting, as we'll see in the next chapter.

If you're interested in exploring further the theme of IT vs the construction industry, there is a whole book on the subject, entitled "IT Success! – towards a new model for Information Technology" (see "Further reading" in Appendix 2).

Funding options for projects and applications

Once projects and applications have been approved during the investment planning phase and made part of the IT budget, how should they be funded from a practical perspective? Should the entire project budget be made available at the start of the year, or should it be released incrementally based on progress milestones? For applications, should new, unplanned work requests, enhancements and scope changes which arise during the year be automatically funded, or would they have to go through an approval process? Let's try and answer these questions.

Applications

For small change requests, feature requests, emergency fixes, etc, which concern production systems, the resulting decision-making process should correspond to the nature of the business problem – and plain common sense. So we clearly want to avoid a top-heavy approval process whose cycle times and effort will probably be as great as the time taken to do the work. Funding for such work is therefore best achieved by drawing from a budget envelope, similar to a current account or cheque account. The amount would be fixed as part of the annual planning process – eg, $100k for Application A, and $500k for Applications B, C and D. The account is then decremented until it runs out.

More significant changes and upgrade requests would of course go through an approval process, not just to obtain the additional – often non-negligible – funding, but also to evaluate the impact on other work and on resource capacity. Approval would therefore result in additional funding over and above the initial application budget, which would either be drawn from some other budget, or from previously approved work which would have to be de-prioritized.

Projects

The most common way of funding a project is to make the complete budget available for the financial year – and sometimes for the whole project if it spans multiple years – based on the business case and the high-level project plan. In essence, funding is given in exchange for commitments on deliverables, costs and schedules. Of course things rarely work out as intended, as we are duly reminded each year by the Standishes of this world when they publish their annual statistics on IT project-success rates (discussed further in Chapter 4).

As explained by the commitment conundrum earlier in this chapter (see Fig. 2.6), it is not possible to accurately determine costs, benefits and risk during the investment-planning process. Realistically, these can only be estimates. It therefore follows that the business case will also be an estimate. It is also not possible to get contractual commitment from the customer in terms of signed-off requirements, since these are yet to be defined. It therefore logically follows that an IT department or an ESP cannot contractually commit to deliverables, costs and schedules – but this is usually done anyway, since that is the "business model" most IT departments and ESPs work to.

So how would we fund projects in such a situation? One answer is to use incremental funding. For large projects, funding is best done based on 3-6 month milestones that recognize uncertainty and the evolving nature of costs, benefits and risk. Examples of milestones would be proof of concept, pilot, first phase with basic deliverables, second phase with additional deliverables, etc. Using this approach a project that did not deliver acceptable benefits at acceptable costs at a given milestone could see its funding postponed, suspended or even cancelled. This should not be seen in a negative light, but simply as part of the reality of delivering IT solutions, which is an organizational learning process out of which you might get some things that work well, and others that work less well and need to be revisited. This would be similar to the way venture capitalists fund requests from entrepreneurs, through incremental funding based on the results of milestones in the business plan. In this way, they are better able to balance risk and return, rather than literally bet a lump sum on an untried and untested plan.

For a further discussion of this venture-capitalist funding approach, please refer to the article entitled "No Crystal Ball for IT" (see "Further reading" in Appendix 2).

IT budget ownership – centralized or decentralized?

The IT budget can be either centralized as part of a corporate cost centre (ie, IT is "free" for the various business customers, since they don't pay for it directly) or charged back in the form of allocations or cross-charges (ie, the business customers pay directly for IT, whose costs figure on their P&Ls). Sometimes both options are possible – eg, common infrastructure and common application costs can be borne centrally as a cost of doing business, and BU-specific applications can be charged back.

Companies charge back IT costs either for financial reasons (eg, for cost recovery or because of corporate policies that require all costs to be transferred to BUs) or as a lever to help balance supply and demand (by eliminating the "free-lunch" syndrome whereby buyers will naturally tend to ask for more when they are not the final payers).

Chapter 3

Cost Management

"One of the soundest rules to remember when making forecasts is that whatever is to happen is happening already." (Sylvia Porter)

Cost management objectives

Cost management allows the IT department to account for how money is being spent in terms of:

- amount (how much?)
- cost categories (on what?)
- cost drivers (by which projects, applications and services?)
- customers (for whom is the money being spent?).

Cost management is both backward-looking (what was spent, or actuals) and forward-looking (how much remains to be spent, or forecasting). Mostly, but not always, cost management is with respect to a budget.

Effective cost management allows a company to keep costs under control, to justify expenditure (actuals with respect to budget) and to make informed decisions about future funding (forecasting).

Capturing IT costs

We saw in Chapter 2 that IT Projects, applications and services result in the following cost categories:

- Hardware
- Software
- People
- External services
- T&E
- Overhead

These costs are captured via a combination of purchasing, time entry and expense reports, which we will discuss in detail further on. Note that we will not discuss activity-based costing (ABC) as a way of capturing costs, because it is not applicable to projects, only to applications or services (see Glossary in Appendix 1 for a discussion on ABC).

We also saw that based on accounting rules, these costs will be either opex, hitting current-year operating expense (eg, people working on data migration); or capex, resulting in annual depreciation (eg, enterprise software licenses).

IT cost drivers

It's one thing to capture costs and know how much was spent in each cost category, but it is also important to understand which projects, applications or customers are generating these costs. This will enable a company to justify IT expenditure, facilitate pricing and chargebacks, or explore opportunities for cheaper alternatives.

Costs should therefore be directly attributed to a cost centre, activity or customer (direct costs), or apportioned based on some form of usage criteria (indirect costs).

Fig. 3.1 shows how the various cost categories can be part of either direct costs, indirect costs, or both.

DIRECT COSTS
(directly attributed to an activity or customer)

DIRECT COSTS (directly attributed to an activity or customer)		INDIRECT COSTS (allocated based on usage or other criteria)
Linked to projects through expense reporting.	**T & E**	
Linked to projects through time entry, for both internal and external staff.	**PEOPLE** • internal staff • contractors • consultants	
Desktop software and certain types of enterprise software licenses and maintenance (eg CRM), can be assigned directly to a customer or department.	**SOFTWARE** • licenses • maintenance • in-house dev	Other types of enterprise software (eg ERP) and in-house developed software are allocated to departments or BUs based on usage or other criteria.
Personal hardware like desktops, laptops and mobile devices can be assigned directly to a customer or department.	**HARDWARE** • servers • networks • equipment	Hardware and infrastructure running enterprise software (eg ERP, CRM) are allocated to departments or BUs based on usage or other criteria.
Certain cloud computing services can be directly assigned to a project (eg PaaS) or a customer (SaaS).	**SERVICE** • telecoms • outsourcing • cloud computing	External services like telecoms, outsourcing and certain cloud computing services (eg IaaS) are allocated to departments or BUs based on usage or other criteria.
	IT OVERHEAD	IT overhead is allocated based on organizational critiera.

Figure 3.1 The IT cost stack – capturing direct and indirect costs

Let us now run through the three main ways of capturing IT costs: through purchasing, time entry and expense reporting.

Purchasing – from POs to invoicing

The purchasing process in most IT departments is usually based on the standard cycle of purchase requisition -> PO -> receiving -> invoicing (see Glossary in Appendix 1 for explanations).

When raising a purchase request, it is important to correctly assign the line items to the appropriate capex or opex account. ERP systems can be automatically set up to do this for unambiguous things like physical goods (eg servers = capex). Unfortunately, this is not always possible for services delivered by contractors, consulting companies or integrators, which can be capex or opex.

So sometimes the accounts have to be selected manually, and this will depend on how understandable the account descriptions are – and on the level of financial awareness of the person raising the requisition. If people in IT who raise requisitions don't know how their actions influence capex and opex – and what capex and opex are in the first place – then you can't really blame them for making mistakes. The chances of error are far from negligible, even for basic purchases like consulting or software licenses. And they could become more problematic for complex POs, for example a "Design and Build" milestone payment that should be set up as say, 70% capex and 30% opex. And when the milestone is reached, the receiving should be done as two separate line items.

One could argue that these concerns are perhaps overkill for what is essentially an upstream process – after all, from a strictly accounting perspective, it would only matter once the invoice was paid and the purchase hit the books. But a combination of insufficient staffing and process inefficiencies makes it highly likely that a PO created with the incorrect accounts will go all the way through to invoicing without being detected. Does your organization have a gatekeeper at the end of the line to catch such mistakes? Probably not.

Time entry – the devil in the detail

Ah, time entry, the subject we all love to hate! By the end of this chapter though, you might come to hate it less – or at least come to terms with it.

On the surface, time entry seems quite simple. People have costs and they work on activities linked to projects, applications and services. So all they have to enter is how much time they worked on the various activities – and that's it. If only things were that simple! Let's take a look at the devil in the detail.

Time entry based on actual hours worked or 8-hour days?

One of first questions to ask about time entry is whether people should enter their time based on actual hours worked, or on a standard working day (usually 8 hours). A standard working day is certainly the easiest from an administrative perspective, but it fails to capture your real costs. So if a project or task was wrongly budgeted, or if unplanned events result in changes, people might have to work 10-hour days instead. If your reporting does not reflect this, then neither will your costs, so you or someone else might make the same wrong estimates on a similar project in the future.

Entering actual hours worked would give you the true cost picture, but might require the introduction of overtime. It could even result in your going over budget if you did your estimates based on 8-hour days with no contingency.

Here's another example. If a person works 8 hours on project A and 2 hours on project B, and his costs are based on a flat rate of 8 hours/day, should he even bother entering the time he spent on project B? After all, it wouldn't change his costs for the day. The answer, of course, is "yes, he should", otherwise project B would have 2 "free" hours of work that would not show up in any reporting.

Finally, time entry has to comply with country labour laws – see next point.

Taking into account legal working-time limits

Some European countries have official working weeks of less than 40 hours. While in some countries this rule is strictly observed, in others people routinely work longer – but the time entry system cannot show this!

Cost rates for internal resources

Companies at a low level of cost-management maturity get by with a single, average internal cost rate for all resources, which is used both for budgeting and for time entry.

The advantage, of course, is simplicity and reduced administration; once defined for the year, the same rate applies to everyone. The obvious disadvantage is that people's activities do not reflect their true cost – after all, a developer does not cost the same as a project manager, and this difference can be amplified based on technologies and experience. This can result in higher or lower costs when compared with real rates. For example, if the average internal rate is say, $600/day, then a developer whose actual rate should be say, $500/day, would result in a higher cost for development. And since development and testing account for most people costs in a project, the overall project cost would be higher than what it should be. Similarly, the project manager who should cost say, $700/day, would result in lower project-management costs.

Comparisons with external contractors and consultants are also skewed. So if a marketing user needs a report that requires 1 week of work from an external resource which she knows she can get for $400/day, but the IT department proposes an internal resource at a standard rate of $600/day, she could claim that the IT department is too expensive.

At the other end of the scale, we would have real rates based on an individual resource's actual, fully-loaded internal cost. Unfortunately, the financial advantages of real costs would soon be outweighed by the complexity and administrative overhead of managing them for dozens or hundreds of people. Even with the automation proposed by time entry systems, the financial accuracy would not be worth the effort.

The compromise solution proposed – and used by companies at a high level of cost management maturity – is to use average cost rates by role, such as developer daily rate or project manager daily rate. Needless to say, this is only feasible when supported by a Management Accounting System (MAS) – see the Glossary in Appendix 1 for an explanation – able to identify the role of the person entering his time.

In the sample budget of Fig. 2.5a, internal staff costs use role-based rates for a UK-based project manager, a France-based

Business Analyst and a US-based Business Analyst.

External resources – time entry or invoicing?

If a contractor works full-time on a project based on a flat daily rate, should her costs be captured through time entry (later reconciled with invoicing), or would it be enough to simply book the monthly invoice against the project code? As discussed earlier in this section, time entry would be the preferred option because it captures the actual time worked and hence the real costs, even though the invoicing would still be based on the flat daily rate.

When external resources do time entry, your purchasing processes should be robust enough to ensure that there is no double-booking of costs, through both time entry and invoicing. These things happen, and people don't always pick up on it.

Overtime, weekend and public holiday rates

What rates would you use for people who work overtime, on weekends, or on public holidays? Would the time-entry system be able to determine what constitutes overtime and to identify public holidays?

How do you ensure timely and accurate time entry?

As if all of the above weren't enough, how do you get people to enter their time accurately (against the correct activities or tasks) and on a regular basis (ideally daily for best accuracy, else at the latest weekly)? We all know people dislike time entry, mainly because they tend to see it, at best, as an administrative tool for management reporting, and at worst, as a policing tool for tracking employee performance. We should hardly be surprised, since probably no one has ever explained to them the financial reasons behind time entry.

When it comes to the approval of time entry, even managers are in the same boat. Some might be more concerned with how many hours their people have worked on a particular project or application, and pay less attention to the underlying tasks or activities, which behind the scenes drive capex and opex.

Are you able to validate all time entry before the monthly close?

Are all of the above processes sufficiently well-honed for you to be able to get all time entry approved and validated in time for the monthly close – or do you require a cut-off period one week earlier? In the latter case, your overall monthly actuals will be mixing apples and oranges – eg, purchasing and other costs on a monthly basis combined with time entry costs on a 3-week basis.

Integrated time entry and project reporting – the holy grail

People working on projects need to account for their time not just for financial-reporting reasons as explained above, but also for project-management reasons, so that project managers can calculate the Estimate to Complete (ETC) for tasks and adjust the plan if required.

People working on projects therefore sometimes have to enter their time twice – once in a time-entry system for the finance and costing side, and again in a project management tool for the project-plan side. Unless, of course, there is some integration between the tools – or better still, if it is a single tool that is capable of meeting both the costing and the project-plan requirements.

Such integrated time-entry and project-management tools do exist (see "How tools can help" in Chapter 5), but they are not often used in this way because:

- All of the process challenges discussed above would have to be adequately addressed so that both the finance department and project managers can work off the same numbers to a sufficiently high degree of confidence. Depending on the organizational balance of power, the finance department provides the numbers to the project managers, or the project managers provide the numbers to the finance department.

- External resources working on projects (large projects are rarely 100%-staffed with internal resources) probably wouldn't be familiar with the tool and would require training. Additional software licenses might also be required.

- No matter how good such tools are, their project-management features and ease of use are usually no match for the ubiquitous Microsoft Project, which most people are familiar with.

So, in practice, integrated time entry and project reporting remains the exception. Either people enter their time twice in two systems, or they do so in one system:

- The time-entry system, where cost management dominates and project managers either accept those numbers or find other ways to calculate ETC.

- The project management system, where project management dominates, and the finance department either accepts the resulting resource costs or finds other ways of calculating them.

In summary

Time entry can be a fairly complex business. Needless to say, except for small projects, using Excel is probably not an option. You will need a professional time-entry system, either a dedicated one or a comprehensive IT management accounting system, with an integrated time-entry module – eg, PPM or PSA (Professional Services Automation) software – ideally interfaced to the financial accounting system.

And even once you've got the mechanics under control, you still have to ensure that people actually enter their time in an accurate and timely manner, and that their managers ensure they are booking their time to the correct tasks or activities, so that the costs are correctly assigned to capex or opex.

Expense reporting – the island of automation

In most companies, IT-related T&E expenses are captured like all other expenses: in the standard company-wide expense-reporting system. This is usually a module of the financial-accounting system, in which it is possible to assign a project code against an expense report or a line item.

This limited granularity makes it difficult to track T&E costs against additional criteria like project phase or activity type, thus making it impossible to assign the costs to capex or opex. So T&E inevitably ends up as opex, since few companies can cost-justify doing this manually. Fortunately, with the exception of international projects with huge travel budgets, this error is usually not significant.

Actuals, accruals and commitments

In an ideal world, all costs incurred in a given month are recognized at the end of that month, so that they can be compared against the budget for that month. In the real world, of course, not all timesheets are approved by month-end and contractors and vendors usually invoice one or two months later (many of them have the same cost-management challenges as the average IT department ...).

So after the monthly close, if you relied only on actuals, your remaining budget would be wrong. So how do you ensure that your budget reflects reality at the start of the next month? The answer is through commitments, or accruals, or a combination of the two. Both commitments and accruals represent uninvoiced work that has already been done, but accruals are actually recorded in the financial accounting system. (Commitments and accruals are explained in detail in the Glossary in Appendix 1).

The true budget situation at the end of each month is therefore: Remaining Budget = Original Budget − (Actuals + Commitments + Accruals).

The challenges of capturing the various costs

Some costs are easy to capture, such as recurring service costs. Others, like people costs, are more challenging. These costs can be captured at different intervals: weekly (eg, time entry), monthly (eg, expense reports) or annually (eg, depreciation).

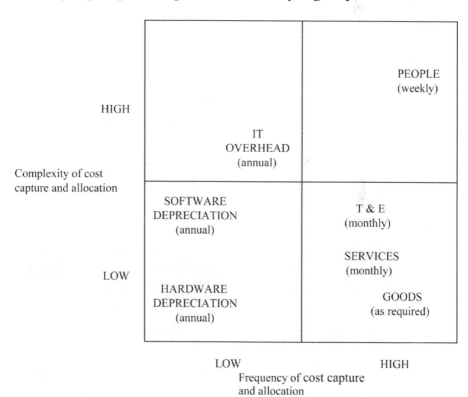

Figure 3.2 Complexity vs frequency - IT costs and allocations

Fig. 3.2 shows the challenges in capturing these various costs as a function of their complexity and the frequency with which they need to be tracked. For example, weekly people costs are the most difficult to capture – and represent in proportion the largest cost category in a project or application budget. IT cost-management efforts should therefore, logically, focus on getting this right first.

Forecasting

Did you ever get hit by a serious cost overrun mid-year into a project, which you never saw coming? And the business sponsor then has to go to the investment committee, cap in hand (capex in hand?), to ask for for money? If so, the chances are there was little or no forecasting taking place.

As mentioned at the start of this chapter, cost management is not just about looking into the past to see how much was spent, but also about looking into the future to estimate remaining costs – at the very minimum for the rest of the financial year, and ideally over a rolling 12-month period (called a rolling forecast).

So actuals should always be accompanied by a forecast, which is the sum of YTD actuals plus estimated remaining spend – in short, an ongoing budget.

Fig. 3.3 represents the sample budget of Fig. 2.5b with updated actuals – and commitments and accruals – for January and February. The remaining budget has also been changed, with additional unforeseen travel in March, and an extension of consulting costs into June. The total of actuals plus remaining represents the forecast. Three months into the project therefore, the revised budget – ie, the forecast – is now $825.6k, compared to the original budget of $811.7k. Project budgets change all the time, as the original assumptions meet business and technological realities 6-9 months after the original budget was defined. (See "Project budgets are just estimates – expect them to change" in Chapter 2).

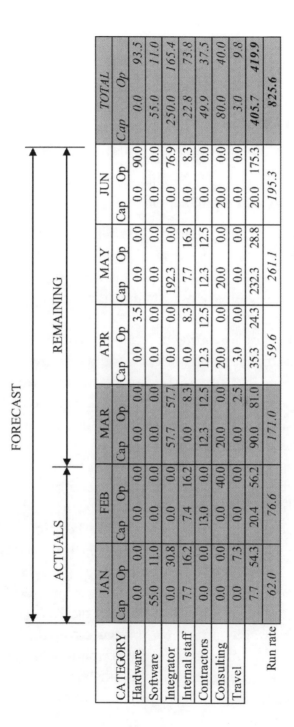

CATEGORY	JAN Cap	JAN Op	FEB Cap	FEB Op	MAR Cap	MAR Op	APR Cap	APR Op	MAY Cap	MAY Op	JUN Cap	JUN Op	TOTAL Cap	TOTAL Op
Hardware	0.0	0.0	0.0	0.0	0.0	0.0	0.0	3.5	0.0	0.0	0.0	90.0	0.0	93.5
Software	55.0	11.0	0.0	0.0	0.0	0.0	0.0	0.0	0.0	0.0	0.0	0.0	55.0	11.0
Integrator	0.0	30.8	0.0	0.0	57.7	57.7	0.0	0.0	192.3	0.0	0.0	76.9	250.0	165.4
Internal staff	7.7	16.2	7.4	16.2	0.0	8.3	0.0	8.3	7.7	16.3	0.0	8.3	22.8	73.8
Contractors	0.0	0.0	13.0	0.0	12.3	12.5	12.3	12.5	12.3	12.5	0.0	0.0	49.9	37.5
Consulting	0.0	0.0	0.0	40.0	20.0	0.0	20.0	0.0	20.0	0.0	20.0	0.0	80.0	40.0
Travel	0.0	7.3	0.0	0.0	0.0	2.5	3.0	0.0	0.0	0.0	0.0	0.0	3.0	9.8
	7.7	54.3	20.4	56.2	90.0	81.0	35.3	24.3	232.3	28.8	20.0	175.3	405.7	419.9
Run rate	62.0		76.6		171.0		59.6		261.1		195.3		825.6	

ACTUALS   FORECAST   REMAINING

Figure 3.3 A sample forecast for the project budget of Fig 2.5b

Timely and accurate forecasting is essential for cost management. Unlike the budgeting and planning phase, which is based on assumptions and estimates, and therefore stands a high chance of being wrong, forecasting is based on what's really happening and is likely to happen. One can even say that for software projects, it is often the budget, and not the spending, that is out of line (see "Project budgets are just estimates – expect them to change" in Chapter 2).

Financial support for cost management

Just as we saw in Chapter 2 when discussing financial support for budgeting, there is no equivalent in IT of "my wife handles the financials". As for budgeting then, you have to essentially handle your own cost management, for which you will need support.

Finance support for budgeting should not be just a one-off exercise limited to annual planning; it should continue throughout the year to ensure that cost management and forecasts meet the same requirements for budget realism and financial compliance. It could even be argued that the requirements for ongoing financial support are greater here; when reality hits during the year, and the inevitable slippages and unplanned spend occur, a combination of organizational pressure and performance incentives could result in a tendency to camouflage reality.

As for budgeting, then, there should be proper financial support and internal controls to ensure that forecasting is realistic and meets financial-compliance guidelines. At a minimum, some sort of financial review board should revisit all major project and application budgets on a quarterly basis.

Without this, the scope for budget overruns and non-compliance is high. This can occur by accident (normal, since IT budget owners are not financial specialists) or design (there's nothing easier than shifting opex to capex if no one is watching...).

The tell-tale sign of inadequate financial support for cost management is when mid-way through the year some project or application suddenly requires serious additional funding – and the financial controllers and IT financial analysts didn't see it coming and are presented with a *fait accompli*.

Understandable cost categories for the business

The various cost components in Fig. 3.1 might be understandable to IT, but they are probably not very meaningful to the business. Regardless of whether IT is a corporate cost centre or whether chargebacks are in place, the various cost categories need to be presented in an understandable format to the business.

This is probably easiest for services, most of which the payer can relate to – eg, "equip a new hire with a laptop and a mobile phone" or "Blackberry mail service".

Unfortunately, this is not possible for projects and applications, which is where most of the costs lie. A CFO or BU manager, for example, is not interested in the details of hardware, software and networks, nor the time spent by various categories of people doing analysis, coding or testing. Costs should therefore be rolled up into three or four understandable categories that anyone can relate to, for example:

- *Product development*, which covers software development, software licenses and software maintenance costs – both during the project phase and for ongoing application maintenance. While IT usually separates the two, not just financially but also organizationally, the customer doesn't care. All he sees are annual costs, period.

- *Infrastructure*, which covers the costs of the physical hardware, system software and networking on which applications and services run.

- *Operations*, which covers the day-to-day running and support costs.

General IT overhead could either be included in an additional catch-all category called *Other*, or be implicitly built into the above three categories.

This type of cost breakdown makes it easier to track application costs from a lifetime perspective, which we shall now consider.

From annual costs to lifetime costs

Since 20% of the average IT budget is for projects and 80% for production applications, it follows that today's projects are tomorrow's applications, and their operating costs over a 5-8 year lifetime consume on average 5 times the original project investment – which explains the 80/20 ratio. When you really think about it, a project is nothing more than the short development phase of a very long application life cycle.

Costs should therefore be tracked from the initial project phase through the entire application life cycle – right through to its retirement.

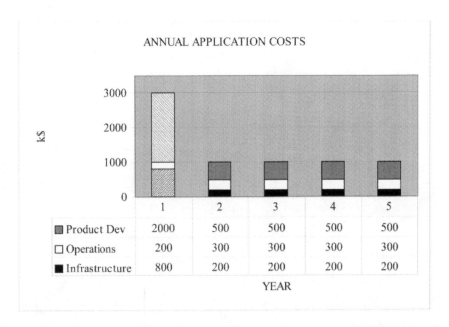

ANNUAL APPLICATION COSTS

	1	2	3	4	5
Product Dev	2000	500	500	500	500
Operations	200	300	300	300	300
Infrastructure	800	200	200	200	200

YEAR

Figure 3.4 Annual application costs

Fig. 3.4 shows the annual costs of an application that was developed in year 1, put in production in year 2 and straight-line depreciated over a 4-year period till its retirement at the end of year 5. To better introduce the concept of annual application costs, this example has been voluntarily over-simplified. There is thus no ongoing maintenance or upgrades, no infrastructure changes, and support costs are constant over the 4-year life span. Note that:

- From an accounting perspective, the only Year 1 costs are $200k opex for operations. The remaining $2.8m represents capital costs, which will be depreciated from Year 2 onwards: $800k for infrastructure and $2m for product development. The capex is shown in a different colour to illustrate that even though the costs will only be depreciated from Year 2 onwards, the company still has to have this cash on hand to pay the vendors for the software licenses and the hardware. The "cash out" for Year 1, which is the sum of capex and opex, is $3m.

- All costs from Year 2 through Year 5 are opex. Operations costs ($300k) are incurred in the course of each year, whereas product development ($500k) and infrastructure costs ($200k) are depreciation expenses obtained by dividing the total Year 1 capital costs by the 4-year depreciation period.

- From the start of Year 2, assuming constant annual operations costs, the *annual application costs are fixed in advance*, since the depreciation expenses for product development and infrastructure *have* to run for 4 years. If, for whatever reason, the system were decommissioned before the end of its useful life, the operations costs would stop right away, but the remaining depreciation expenses would still be "owed", and would therefore have to be written off – ie, expensed to the current financial year. (See "Write off" in the Glossary in Appendix 1, which explains this in more detail).

In the real world, of course, applications have maintenance, upgrades and variable operations costs, so the costs would actually increase over time in a step-wise fashion (not shown).

Combining costs and benefits

With a clear view on annual application costs, the logical next step would be to measure application benefits over the same period, which would enable a cost-benefit approach.

When quantifiable, benefits can be either be defined in financial terms – eg, various Return on Investment (ROI) measures like Net Present Value (NPV) or Internal Rate of Return (IRR). Benefits can also be defined in operational terms, such as sales cycle-, delivery- or customer-service performance. Ideally, you should be able to translate this into increased revenue or decreased costs, but in practice this is extremely difficult – you can never be sure to what extent changes in benefits are linked to the application, or to other factors.

Let's see how we could combine costs and benefits for the application example of Fig. 3.4 above. If this application is supposed to deliver the operational benefit of shorter order cycle time, the values could be plotted annually and superimposed onto Fig. 3.4. Such a combined costs-and-benefits chart (not shown) would immediately show how annual application funding is actually contributing to decreasing order cycle time.

Monitoring application costs and benefits from a lifetime perspective and rolling them up into a portfolio, is called Application Portfolio Management (APM). APM allows a company to evaluate for each application the return on the initial investment (in financial or operational terms) and whether ongoing funding is justified – or if the application should be targeted for retirement.

Fig. 3.5a shows an example of an application portfolio for the Sales & Marketing Operations of a BU, with the breakdown of spend for 2010. Fig. 3.5b shows the history over the past 5 years. The increasing annual costs can be explained by a combination of the changing business environment (eg, increased hiring or a product launch) – or by poorly performing applications. For example, drilling down on the corresponding application – eg, SFA, in the pie chart of Fig. 3.5a, or the histogram of Fig. 3.5b – should show the corresponding cost-benefit analysis as discussed above.

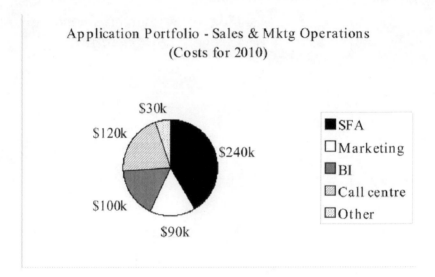

Figure 3.5a Example of an application portfolio – prior year costs

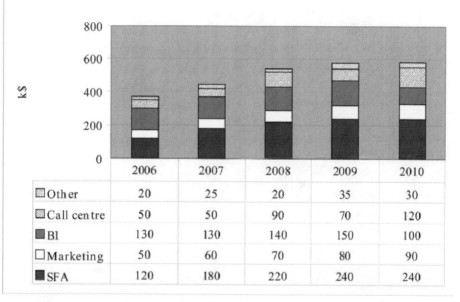

Figure 3.5b Example of an application portfolio – costs for last five years

Chapter 4

Chargebacks

"The pen is mightier than the sword, but no match for the accountant." (Jonathan Glancey)

An emotionally charged subject

As explained at the end of Chapter 2, the IT budget can be centralized as part of a corporate cost centre, or charged back to BUs so that both costs and benefits sit on their P&Ls – or a combination of the two.

Chargebacks can be a relatively complex – and emotionally charged – subject for both BUs and IT, and need to be entered into with caution, with an initial over-emphasis on simplicity and buy-in as opposed to bean counting and the potential for rejection. What you're ultimately looking for is not strict financial accuracy, but workable results in terms of cost recovery or regulating demand through adequate pricing. The challenge is to strike the right balance between the desired result (fair and reasonably accurate) and the costs and complexity of obtaining actual, metered usage.

Once you've decided on chargebacks and which cost categories have to be borne by the client, you then have to put in place a mechanism for transferring these costs from IT to the business. This can be done through a combination of allocations and cross-charging.

Allocations

Allocations take the costs of shared infrastructure and applications software and spread them over BUs based on one or more criteria such as headcount, revenue or actual usage. While actual usage is the most objective criteria, it can be taken to extremes and become horrendously expensive and complex in practice. It therefore needs to be entered into with caution. Allocations are usually rolled into BU overhead at the start of the financial year, with a year-end adjustment to take into account actuals.

Besides the challenges of finding transparent and objective criteria – as opposed to a voodoo formula – allocations suffer from the key disadvantage of being relatively invisible to those whose behaviour they are supposed to influence. Because they are often buried in annual overhead, they are usually not adequately communicated to the actual application users who make requests for IT products and services – indeed, they might not even be aware that their department is paying for IT. That is why it makes better sense to do cost allocations at as detailed a level as possible (ideally, down to the departmental and application level), so that the resulting costs have a chance of influencing user behaviour.

Cross-charging

For projects and applications, cross-charging takes the costs of human resources (internal or external) and charges them directly to the customer, based on their cost rate. For services, these costs would be rolled up into understandable terms for the business – eg, "Application ABC support services". Cross-charging is ideally done on a monthly basis, or at the very least, quarterly.

When an IT department is a separate business entity or subsidiary that provides shared services to BUs, as opposed to an internal or corporate department, then the term invoicing, rather than cross-charging, is used. Such BUs would receive invoices from IT in exactly the same way as they receive invoices from vendors or ESPs. Apart from that, there is no difference between cross-charging and invoicing, and the terms are often used interchangeably.

Cross-charges have the advantage of visibility and regularity – they land on your desk every month and are thus more likely to generate the desired behaviour necessary to regulate demand. This is especially true if – and there are tools which allow you to do this – the level of detail goes down to the actual user and the associated work, instead of just being rolled up to the departmental or BU level ("Hey Joe – that new report you asked for last month has ended up costing quite a bit. Was it really that important...?").

Customer transparency – the bare essentials

When we receive our monthly utility bills or credit-card statements, we expect them to be understandable, accurate and fair. We also need to know, explicitly or implicitly, prior costs and likely future trends, all of which helps us to evaluate whether we are getting a good deal or not. If any of these requirements are not met, we then start to query the service and, in a worst case scenario, we leave for the competition. The same is true for IT chargebacks – except that it's difficult to leave for the competition. (Well, you could always try ...).

The bare essentials in terms of transparency – no pun intended – is being able to answer the following questions from a customer:

- What am I paying for?

- What am I getting out of it?

- How have my costs been increasing or decreasing over the past few years?

- What are my projected costs for the next few years?

This sounds reasonable enough, but as we shall now see, not many IT departments are able to do this.

Chargebacks – the devil in the detail

Just as we saw for time entry in Chapter 3, on the surface, chargebacks seem quite simple. As long as we are able to accurately capture our project-, application- and service costs, all we have to do is bill them to the customer – period. And as for time entry, if only things were that simple! Let's take a look at the devil in the detail.

How understandable are chargebacks?

Clarity and ease of understanding are the first things one notices in an invoice. They go a long way in influencing your trust in a vendor – even if further examination might later reveal the contents to be inaccurate or unfair.

Unfortunately, chargebacks are usually characterized by incomprehensible line items in an Excel dump, whose granularity can vary from the lowest-level journal entry from the general accounting system, to a terse one-liner with the application or service description.

When it comes to chargebacks, you cannot excel with Excel. Unclear and confusing invoices are the thin edge of the wedge – they virtually guarantee that the contents will be queried, which can potentially lead to the whole chargeback model being put under the spotlight.

The only cost-effective way around this is to have monthly invoicing produced from a management-accounting system, with a consolidated view of allocations and cross-charges.

In addition to monthly invoices, customers should also get an annual snapshot similar to Figs 3.5a and 3.5b, so that they can see the historic trend in their application costs and benefits, as well as projected costs for the next few years.

Are costs accurate enough for chargebacks?

We saw in Chapter 3 the challenges in capturing IT costs, and why there is such a high margin of error in the numbers. This was confirmed by the PSB poll mentioned in the Introduction, which showed that up to 75% of respondents estimate a margin of error of 5-20% in their actual costs.

If IT is a corporate cost centre, this margin of error remains an internal problem. If, however, the numbers are ultimately charged back to BUs, then that changes things completely. If a customer feels "beyond reasonable doubt" that there is inaccuracy in your costing, then that puts your whole chargeback model under the spotlight ("If your costs for application ABC or service XYZ are inaccurate, how can I trust the rest of your pricing?").

The risks to IT credibility and the potential organizational fallout that would result from the exposure of unacceptably inaccurate chargeback costs should be the main driver for IT to get its house in order when it comes to capturing costs. Realistically, an IT department should be able to demonstrate – and not just declare – a margin of error for costs of less than 10%, otherwise it would be leaving its chargeback underbelly exposed.

How fair are cost allocation models?

The most common way of apportioning indirect costs is to use the criterion of headcount, or number of users. These are chosen not because they are necessarily fair, but because they're the easiest to implement.

The main assumption with headcount, or with number of users, is that usage is equivalent across BUs. While this might be sufficiently true for things like desktop services, which everyone must use, it is not true for most business applications. The reason is that it does not distinguish between light and heavy usage, nor does it expose what's driving the usage. For example, when it comes to expensive CRM licenses, it might not be fair to ask an office-based marketing assistant to pay the same as a field-based sales rep – especially if a BU was able to obtain variable pricing on the market.

OK, so let's consider bringing usage or consumption into the equation. Physical machine time is best left out of the picture, not only because it is difficult to calculate, but because it has no relevance to the customer (MIPS might stand for Millions of Instructions per Second to IT, but for the business, it might as well stand for Meaningless Indicator of Processor Speed). Usage based on business-relevant transactions is far better – eg, number of leads, orders or customer calls processed monthly by an application. But even here, the law of unintended consequences could apply. For example, low usage of a CRM system by sales reps would generate low chargebacks – hardly a good management incentive when rep usage is one of the biggest challenges in CRM! Similarly, allocating call-centre costs by measuring the number of customer calls could end up penalizing the more successful products that are generating the most customer calls.

BU revenue might seem a fairer allocation criterion – or is it? Shouldn't it also take into account productivity? Otherwise it penalizes high-performance BUs and rewards the low-performing ones. So BU revenue per employee would be a fairer measure. But wait, you might say – what about external staff? So BU revenue by total number of people, internal and external, would be even fairer. But hang on – what about capital ratios? A BU might have fewer people but higher capital costs through fixed assets? We wouldn't want them to get a free ride, would we? And so you can go on and on to make it fairer – but at what cost in complexity and administration?

A simple but effective step up from the headcount model is to add a burden rate or consumption factor for a BU for a given project, application or service. This would be based on factors ranging from actual or estimated consumption observed over a period of time (eg, prior year) to business drivers like revenue or contribution. This factor would increase or decrease the chargeback amounts to take into account consumption and business realities. An example would be a new BU in an emerging country; it would be not only unfair, but also illogical, to apply the same per-user pricing to a BU in an established market as a new BU in an emerging market in start-up mode. So the start-up BU might have a burden rate of 0.5, effectively halving its costs. These reduced costs would then have to be reallocated against the other BUs if the objective is cost recovery – not a good approach, since you are creating unjustified cost dependencies between BUs that would otherwise have no business dependencies. The preferred solution would be for Corporate to pick up the additional costs as part of the costs of starting up a new BU. Burden rates would be reassessed periodically (eg, every six months or annually).

Another simple but effective option would be to have both fixed and variable costs. For example, desktop services could have a fixed-cost component per user, which would be easily defendable. An example is one based on software licenses and basic services on a flat fee, use-it-or-lose-it basis. There would then be additional variable costs based on consumption above a certain threshold (eg, disk space or Blackberry e-mail).

In conclusion, a lot of thought needs to go into allocation models to come up with something that is fair, reasonably accurate and cost-effective in terms of administrative effort. Probably the recommended minimum would be to build on the simplistic headcount or per-user model by adding a burden rate or a consumption rate.

How do allocations take into account project risk?

Most people in IT are aware of the statistics concerning IT project success rates, which, even in the 21st century, still sit stubbornly at around one in three. Or, to deliberately take the negative view, two out of every three IT projects are unsuccessful. For example, the Standish "CHAOS Summary 2009" reports the following project success statistics:

- *Successful* – "32% delivered on time, on budget, with required features and functions."

- *Challenged* – "44% were challenged, which are late, over budget and/or with less than required features and functions."

- *Failed* – "24% failed (cancelled prior to completion, or delivered and never used)."

It's not sure that the BUs who have to pay for projects are aware of these statistics. If they were, they would logically ask for the risk to be shared, either with other BUs or with Corporate. And failing that, they would step back and let some other BU go first with any new project.

As for high-risk, high-reward, strategic initiatives that could bring significant competitive differentiation (see "Portfolio-based investment planning" in Chapter 2), these might simply never be launched if no BU is willing to take the financial risk and be on the bleeding edge of technology.

So the natural question is "who should bear project risk before it becomes (if it becomes...) a production application – BUs, Corporate or IT?". The logical answer would be "not the BUs". The recommended approach is to share the risks and the funding between the BUs, and either Corporate or IT. This could also be combined with "scorecard relief", so that project costs do not affect BU financial performance.

Once the project has gone live – *and* has stabilized as a production application, usually not before one year – subsequent running costs can then be charged back to the BUs.

A general rule of thumb is that if a company wants to encourage experimentation of a new technology, or adoption of a new system, then there should be little or no chargebacks, and costs should be borne centrally. Once technologies are mature, or new systems adopted, then chargebacks should be introduced to manage demand and allocate costs based on usage.

How do you account for non-chargeable activities?

Not all time that internal staff spend can be directly allocated to projects, applications or services. Without even talking about general overhead associated with things like management, facilities and career development (which in any case applies to the whole company), there are some very specific IT activities that are difficult, if not impossible, to directly charge back to a BU. Examples are "pre-sales" and "account management" – in other words the customer interaction time spent in meetings, demand management, evaluating opportunities, performing estimates and evaluations for work ranging from simple reports to major projects. Some of these will eventually become reality, but most will not. In the outside world, these activities are sometimes explicitly billed, or more often built into the price of products and services. Even if customers don't always like this, they do understand it, since nobody works for free.

Capturing these types of activities through time entry is easy. The question is what do you do with it afterwards? Some companies realistically factor this into their overhead costs, either to be borne centrally or to be allocated out based on some criteria. Others pretend it doesn't exist – or worse, assume it shouldn't exist – and get their staff to assign all of their time to projects or applications so it can be merged into the rest of the chargebacks.

International projects – you go first!

International projects are frighteningly expensive and fraught with complexity, both technical and organizational. The theory behind cost savings, synergies and process standardization hardly ever materializes, as anyone who has ever managed one can probably attest to. If you now also throw chargebacks into the mix, things can really become messy.

Unless affiliates or countries that are candidates for an international project have some sort of mechanism in place for sharing the risks and the costs with Corporate or with IT, they will end up having to bear *all* of the costs. And this can be really tricky.

Let's take an example of an international CRM project for 1000 users spread across 10 countries. The total costs, from software licenses and infrastructure to integrators and contractors, can easily exceed a few million dollars. If all the costs have to be recovered based on a per-user allocation method, then here are just some of the questions you would have to answer:

- One of the main reasons behind doing an international project is to share the costs. But how would you do so? Should the first countries to go live pay less to take into account project risk? After all, countries coming in on a later release would shoulder far less risk – indeed, they might even decide to delay their implementation based on the results from the first countries. Shouldn't they therefore pay more? Or maybe have an average cost – suitably adjusted by a burden rate for some countries – which would probably be a fairer approach?

- The greater the number of users worldwide, the lower the unit costs. The project therefore has an economic incentive to lock in as many countries as possible to keep chargebacks low. So if a country wanted to opt out of its implementation slot for valid business reasons, and there was no other country ready to take its place, then the total costs for that year would have to be spread across fewer users, resulting in higher costs for the remaining countries. The effect would be magnified if the opt-out country accounted for a large number of users. Would it be acceptable for the other countries to have to pick up the additional costs, or should they be borne centrally so as to not increase the costs they originally committed to?

- If a country wanted to postpone or opt out, as described in the previous point, should it be allowed to do so? Should it pay an "opt-out penalty fee" for the project disruption and the additional costs incurred?

- The first countries to go live will no doubt end up generating more support costs then subsequent countries. How should first-year support costs be allocated?

- From a strictly financial standpoint, depreciation should start once the first countries goes live. After all, most of the capital investment in software licenses and infrastructure will have been made then. But what percentage of the total depreciation should these first countries start paying? Is it realistic from an administrative standpoint to start depreciation like this, or would it be simpler – even if not financially compliant – to have depreciation for all countries start in the following financial year?

As you can see, it really does become rather messy. And we didn't even cover the intricacies of spreading the costs of new versions across those countries that are already live, and across new countries. Or when new versions have expensive features that are only used by a couple of countries, and you have to figure out how to share the costs across all countries.

Clearly, if company financial policy allows it, the best option would be to have international project costs entirely financed centrally. Failing that, it should be financed only partially by the countries in such a way as to eliminate most of the above complexity. For example, project costs could be financed centrally until a critical mass of countries is live and the system is operationally stable. Chargebacks could then kick in to cover ongoing operational costs and – when feasible – part of the ongoing depreciation.

Full cost recovery for international projects is probably the worst option (as you can probably tell, I bear the scars and stripes of real experience…).

Customer questions you should be able to answer

If a BU customer wanted to better understand her invoicing with respect to the bare essentials discussed at the start of this chapter, here are some fundamental questions she would probably ask:

- What am I paying for?

- What am I getting out of it?

- How have my costs been increasing or decreasing over the past few years?

- What are my projected costs for the next few years?

- Do my project, application or service costs include IT overhead, or is this a separate line item? If included, how is it calculated and on what basis is it allocated?

- How do I know I am not subsidizing another BU (or country)?

- What is the margin of error in your costs, and how do I ensure I'm not paying for them? What are you doing about reducing the margin of error?

At the end of the day, IT should be able to walk a customer through its chargeback processes, from how costs are captured to how they are charged back. And to ensure that it isn't just a slick presentation, you should be able to take any cost – eg, last year's desktop service costs or CRM application costs – and show how they were arrived at.

If you are unable to do this, then at best, things will continue as before – but you will have an unsatisfied customer. At worst, she will take up the case with the CFO – or even request an audit of your whole costing model.

Chapter 5

Next Steps

"Nothing in life is static; it either gets better, or it gets worse." (Lloyd Dobens)

Financial maturity assessment

As you get to the end of this book, the logical next step will be to assess your level of financial maturity. The essential questions to ask are "where do I stand today, and what can I do to increase my level of financial awareness – or that of my team, department or organization?"

Fig. 5.1 shows a simple low/medium/high financial maturity scale across the key areas of investment planning, budgeting, cost management and chargebacks.

You can undertake a formal maturity assessment with external help (see "How consultants can help" further on), or you can start with a simple self-assessment by answering the following basic yes/no questions.

Note that strict numeric scores have been deliberately avoided, so that you can focus on what you *feel* your current maturity level is, rather than on what any mathematical score may say. The more your answers are in the negative, the lower will be your financial maturity.

	INVESTMENT PLANNING	BUDGETING	COST MANAGEMENT	CHARGEBACKS
HIGH (Practicing)	• Demand mgt with scoring models and business cases • Annual planning combined with ongoing planning • Portfolio mgt for both projects and applications	• Formal budgeting with strong Finance support • Fully auditable capex/opex budgeting at granular level • 12-month rolling forecasts • Flexible funding options for projects and applications	• Full cost categorization • Reliable time entry • Commitments and accruals • Role-based cost rates • Low margin of error in actuals – less than 10%	• Understandable, fair and reasonably accurate • Full cost visibility, including future trends • Chargebacks fully linked to business benefits • Transparent and auditable
MEDIUM (Developing)	• Account mgt initiatives and the start of demand mgt • Annual planning with clear and rational processes • Categorization of project and application investments	• More reliable budgeting; improved Finance support • Capex/opex rules enforced more rigorously • More reliable forecasting • Project budgets sometimes revisited during the year	• Better cost categorization • Improved time entry • Tracking of commitments • Role-based cost rates • Medium margin of error in actuals – between 10-30%	• More customer-friendly chargebacks • Visibility on both current- and prior year costs • Beginnings of linking costs to business benefits • Improved transparency
LOW (Ad hoc)	• Annual planning done in urgency mode in 1-2 mths • Approvals based mainly on business sponsor influence • Limited categorization of investments	• Ad hoc budgeting; limited support from Finance • Capex/opex budgeting rules difficult to enforce • Little or no forecasting • Contractual project budgets cast in stone	• Limited cost categorization • Error-prone time entry • No commitments tracking • One standard cost rate • High margin of error in actuals – at least 30%	• Complex, inaccurate and generally unfair • No views on prior-year costs or future trends • No relation of costs to business benefits • Opaque and unauditable

Figure 5.1 IT financial maturity levels

Investment planning

1. Do you have a demand management pipeline to enable ongoing planning, or does your planning essentially take place over a 1-2 month period?

2. Are you able to do an opportunity analysis on your demand pipeline based on an appropriate scoring model?

3. Are all project requests supported by a business case based on a combination of business alignment, costs, benefits, technology alignment, risk and IT resource and scheduling constraints?

4. Do you use portfolio management for investment decision-making, or do you primarily use a simple prioritization approach for funding projects and applications?

5. If you do have an IT investment portfolio, does it stay essentially unchanged throughout the year (reflecting contractual commitments to individual business sponsors), or can its composition change depending on changing business objectives, expected return and risk (reflecting an overall organizational approach to investment)?

6. Do you have account managers or business relationship managers whose dedicated role it is to understand and manage – even challenge – customer demand?

Budgeting

1. Do you feel your IT budget owners have the right level of financial awareness to be able to properly define their budgets?

2. Do you feel they get enough financial support – from the finance department or internally from within IT – when defining their budgets?

3. Do you feel they are able to effectively carry out both their day jobs and the budgeting associated with the annual planning process?

4. Do you think their budgets would be able to pass a financial audit in terms of compliance with capex-vs-opex rules?

5. Do you think their budgets would pass an IT best-practice audit in terms of covering all possible aspects of IT costs?

6. Do you have any fail-safe processes (from check-lists to budget-review boards) to monitor financial compliance and to ensure that nothing falls through the cracks – or do you expect the budget owners to "just get the job done and turn in the numbers"?

7. Do you set the expectation to the business and the CFO that project budgets can and will evolve over time, or do they see them as contractually cast in stone?

8. Do you fund major projects entirely for the financial year based on their business case, or do you release funds incrementally based on progress milestones?

9. Are infrastructure costs budgeted as part of projects and applications, or are they part of a separate budget that will be allocated out to the rest of the company?

Cost management

1. Do you feel your IT senior and middle management have the right level of financial awareness to be able to raise requisitions and POs so that the goods or services are correctly assigned to capex or opex?

2. Do you feel that the majority of your people who do time entry understand that they are doing so for financial reasons – with direct capex and opex budget impact – or do they mainly see it as an administrative chore?

3. Do the majority of your people enter their time on a daily or weekly basis, or is it more a month-end activity?

4. Do you use role-based cost rates to track your people costs, or do you use a standard resource cost rate across all profiles, from junior to senior?

5. Does your monthly reporting reliably reflect uninvoiced work (through accruals or commitments)?

6. Do your IT budget owners do regular monthly forecasts, or do they just track actuals and only forecast on an as-needed basis?

7. Do you think their actuals and forecasts would be able to pass a financial audit in terms of compliance with capex vs opex rules?

8. Do you feel they get enough financial support – from the finance department or internally from within IT – to effectively carry out both their day jobs and absorb the administrative overhead associated with effective cost management?

9. Do you think your project and application costs can be put into a form easily understandable by the business (regardless of whether you do chargebacks or not)?

10. Do you track application costs on a lifetime basis, or do you only focus on the current financial year?

11. Do you track applications from a cost-benefit perspective to evaluate the return on the initial project investment and to justify ongoing funding?

12. Do you feel your IT financial controllers and IT financial analysts have the right level of IT awareness to be able to understand – let alone challenge – the actuals and forecasts that they are presented with each month, both in terms of content (cost categories) and in terms of adherence to capex vs opex rules? Or do they simply take the numbers at face value?

Chargebacks

1. Do you feel comfortable using IT actuals in their current form as a basis for chargebacks? Are you satisfied that the margin of error is sufficiently low?

2. Do you feel that your chargeback policies are understandable, reasonably accurate and fair?

3. Do you think you'd be able to satisfactorily answer the fundamental questions a customer is likely to ask

concerning chargebacks (see "Customer questions you should be able to answer" in Chapter 4)?

4. Are your BU customers formally aware of IT project-success statistics, and how does your chargeback model take this into account?

5. Is your chargeback model able to adequately address the challenges of international projects (see "International projects – you go first!" in Chapter 4)

Improving your financial maturity

If most of your replies to the previous questions are in the negative, then you should consider raising the level of financial awareness of your organization and revisiting your financial processes across the affected areas.

To improve your financial maturity, you can either focus on your pain points, or focus on those areas that are already working well – or you might have no choice in the matter:

*   The first and most common approach is to focus on one or more pain points and address those, eg, consistently inaccurate financial reporting in terms of capex and opex, or a highly visible enterprise-wide project with a serious budget overrun that nobody saw coming.

*   The second approach takes the opposite tack to pain points, and actually looks for those areas that are already working well. Most companies will usually have at least one mature group with a well-run project or a stable application. Such a group will by definition already be doing a lot of things right, and increasing their level of financial awareness would be a logical step in their overall process maturity. Once

this group is able to demonstrate the benefits of improved financial maturity in a particular area, it could then become a showcase or catalyst for the rest of the organization.

- Lastly, you might not have any choice in the matter: a failed audit, significantly reduced IT spending or the upcoming migration to a new ERP system are all examples of factors which might require IT to get its house in order on the financial front.

Your starting point can therefore be any one of the above, or a combination, depending on circumstances.

How tools can help

Implementing IT financial management, even on a basic scale, will require the help of a software tool to support the new processes. As discussed in this book when looking at the details of planning, budgeting, cost management and chargebacks, it would really be a challenge to properly manage the end-to-end financial processes on a mix of Excel, Access or in-house developed systems.

Amazingly, today, in an age in which most companies would simply be unable to function without IT to manage its production, sales, delivery and service, the IT department remains the proverbial cobbler's child with no shoes. Whereas the rest of the business like Marketing, Sales, Order Management, Finance, Customer Service – even HR – all have their systems, from stand-alone applications to integrated ERP and CRM, the IT department usually has to make do with Microsoft Project and Excel! And yet, it has to run a business probably just as complex as the rest of the company, one based on products, services, orders, resources, projects, technology, finance and support. This is an aberration, to say the least!

The main reason for this is the lack of appropriate tools and technology, which have come relatively late to IT. These have matured over the past 5-8 years, and there now exists a credible offering of software packages that allows an IT department to "do business" with its customers, both internal and external. They fall mainly into the categories of PPM, PSA and SM software.

As beneficial as these product offerings may be, most of them remain best-of-breed standalone solutions – though some players are starting to put together integrated solutions. There are also vendors in the areas of Billing/Chargeback, Business Performance and Business Intelligence, that attempt to tie it all together. The Forrester report entitled "Market Overview: IT Financial Management Software" (see "Further reading" in Appendix 2) evaluates the ability of these vendors to successfully position themselves in the area of ITFM.

From a financial perspective and within the context of this book, all of these tools fall into the category of Management Accounting Systems (MAS). These are parallel accounting systems that augment the General Accounting System (GAS) to manage costs and revenue based on management criteria like projects, applications and customers.

Ideally, the GAS manages accounting, purchasing and expense reporting – often integrated as part of the ERP system – while the MAS manages projects, applications, services and infrastructure. This ideal situation is shown in Fig. 5.2a, which shows a fully integrated MAS capable of dealing with all operational IT activities and able to generate consolidated chargebacks for the GAS. All the GAS would need to provide to the MAS are actuals from purchasing and expense reporting.

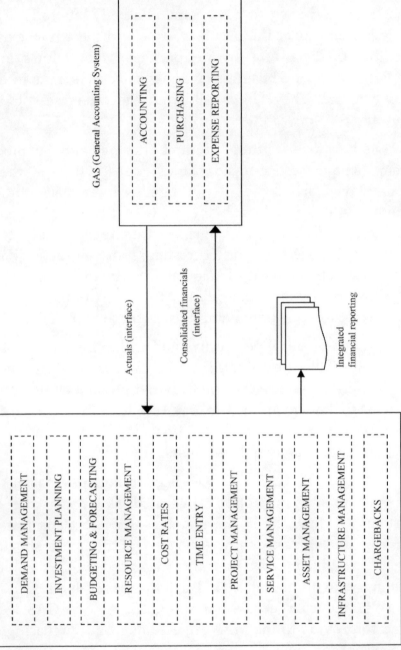

Figure 5.2a Tooling – ideal situation

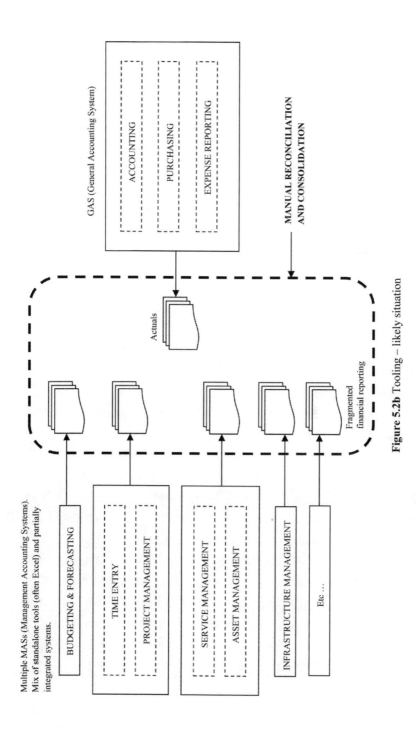

Figure 5.2b Tooling – likely situation

In the real world, of course, such integration is still a good few years away, both in terms of vendor offerings and in terms of integrated processes between IT and Finance. The most likely tooling situation is shown in Fig. 5.2b, which reflects the state of IT financial management today. Until such tool and process integration becomes reality, there is a window of opportunity for the Billing/Chargeback, Business Performance and Business Intelligence vendors that are able to position themselves in the middle and consolidate the multiple MASs into a coherent whole to provide chargeback financials for the GAS.

How consultants can help

Having just made the case for software vendors above, it follows that consultants also need to get a piece of the action.

You will almost certainly require outside assistance in getting from here to there. Unfortunately, there are not many large consulting companies with the expertise to help you carry out a maturity assessment or put together a change programme in IT financials. So you'll probably end up working with small, specialist consulting companies that can demonstrate the requisite IT financials experience.

The exact nature of the change programme will depend on the results of the maturity assessment and the subsequent process improvement objectives. But the chances are high that one of the very first steps will be the introduction of a formal training programme to increase the financial awareness of IT staff across one or more of the key areas of investment planning, budgeting, cost management and chargebacks. Just as for consulting though, don't expect to find many such training programmes on the market. In all probability you will have to work with your chosen consultants to set one up.

Roles and responsibilities

IT financial management requires the following fundamental roles:

- IT Financial Controllers, to support IT financial management processes and to validate all information provided by the various MASs (not just for projects, but also applications, services and infrastructure). IT Financial Controllers are part of the Finance department.

- IT Financial Manager, to design (in conjunction with IT Financial Controllers) and own IT financial management practices across the key areas of investment planning, budgeting, cost management and chargebacks. The IT Financial Manager is part of the IT Department, and normally has a team to run and manage one or more MASs (count 1 or 2 people to run a MAS).

While all companies have IT Financial Controllers (whose knowledge of IT may vary considerably ...), the same unfortunately cannot be said for IT Financial Managers. This simply serves to reinforce the whole premise of this book, which is that despite the size of IT spending, the average CIO does not accord the required priority to financials in her organization.

The costs of implementing IT financial management

Closely linked to any requirement to increase the financial maturity of the IT department would be the costs of change. What would it cost to implement effective IT financial management? What would it cost to *not* do anything and continue as before?

Let's start by answering the second question first because it's the easiest. Depending on your current maturity level, the costs of not doing anything would be a continuation of poor IT financial performance. Examples could be a high margin of error in IT costs, regular budget overruns (due as much to poor budgeting as to poor cost management) unreliable forecasting, incomprehensible chargebacks, unwelcome auditor scrutiny due to financial non-compliance – all the way to the near-certainty that your financial processes and MASs will be earmarked for retirement soon after a merger or acquisition because your financial management practices suck.

The answer to the first question now suddenly becomes quite easy, namely that the costs of implementing sound IT financial practices would pale in comparison to the costs of doing nothing.

If we tried to quantify these costs at a high level, this is what you could expect (with the usual qualifier that these are only estimates and would depend on the maturity of each company):

- Additional heads in Finance to improve support for IT financial processes (count 1 or 2 people).

- Additional heads in IT for the role of IT Financial Manager and his team (count 1 or 2 people).

- Training costs to raise the level of financial awareness of IT, initially at senior- and middle-management level, and later for the whole department (count a series of 2 or 3 hour workshops in one or more of the key areas of investment planning, budgeting, cost management and chargebacks).

- Training costs to raise the level of IT awareness of IT Financial Controllers and their supporting staff (count a 2 or 3 hour workshop on IT basics, from development methodologies to the role of MASs).

- Software licenses, implementation services and running costs for an integrated MAS to support the new financial processes (count $200k to $1m or more depending on the number of users, the level of integration and whether it would be an on-premises investment or a hosted offering).

- Consulting assistance for:

  o an in-depth financial maturity assessment (if required)

  o a change management programme, including the setting up of a training programme adapted to your financial maturity (count 1 or 2 people for 4-6 weeks).

Reader feedback

While things are still fresh in your mind, you might want to share your thoughts and even take part in short surveys on various topics. To do so, please visit my website at www.itprojectfinancials.com.

Appendix 1

Glossary of Common Financial Terms

READING SEQUENCE FOR BEGINNERS: If you are not very familiar with financials, then instead of reading from A-Z, it would make better sense to start in the following sequence:

1. Costs

2. Depreciation

3. Write off

4. Financial Accounting System

5. Management Accounting System

6. Recognition

7. Accruals

8. Commitments

Also note as you read through the explanations that terms in *italics* are part of the glossary.

ABC (Activity-Based Costing): a method for assigning *costs* to products and services based on the activities required to produce them. Knowing how much products and services really cost allow companies to justify expenditure, identify what's profitable vs unprofitable and explore opportunities for cheaper alternatives.

ABC is best understood via an example. Let's imagine a customer service department in a Business-to-Business (B-to-B) telco with a team of multi-skilled call centre agents who handle both external customer enquiries and internal enquiries from the sales force. In addition, they correct orders that have wrong or missing information by calling the customers and doing it on the phone.

You build an ABC model by first interviewing the agents and asking them how much time they spend on these three activities, which they estimate at 60%, 30% and 10% respectively (for simplicity's sake we will avoid breaking down these activities into "cost pools"). You then count the number of "cost drivers" – ie, the number of external enquiries, internal enquiries and rejected orders – which for our example is say, 10 000, 2 500 and 1 000 per year respectively. Finally you factor in the total *costs* of the department, which are $1m per year.

This data is then entered into a model in an ABC system, which calculates the following activity cost driver rates (Fig. 6.1 below):

ACTIVITY	TIME SPENT	COST ($)	COST DRIVER	QTY	ACTIVITY COST DRIVER RATE
Handle external inquiries	60%	600 000	Customer calls	10 000	$60/customer call
Handle internal inquiries	30%	300 000	Sales force calls	2 500	$120/sales force call
Process rejected orders	10%	100 000	Rejected orders	1 000	$100/rejected order
	100%	1 000 000			

Figure 6.1 An example of Activity-Based Costing (ABC)

Needless to say, this simplistic example hides a number of inaccuracies and complexities, the main ones of which are:

- The time spent is based on people's subjective estimates of their behaviour – and assumes 100% annual productivity, with no idle time.

- Any changes in activities and processes due to new or changed products, or to exception processing, would require re-interviewing and maintenance of the model.

- If the approach were applied to 100 people instead of only three, and across multiple activities more complex than those for a call centre, the effort and cost involved in interviewing people, setting up the model and maintaining it could soon become prohibitive.

- If required, as in IT, it would be difficult to break down people's activities into *capex* and *opex*.

The conclusion is that ABC is more suited to relatively stable, industrial, commodity-type processes with little exception processing. It would also need to be a high-volume activity to justify the overhead of maintaining an ABC system.

Even in a stable industrial environment, the above constraints can still become a barrier to ABC, which has led the inventors of the original model, Robert S. Kaplan and Steven R. Anderson, to propose in 2003 a simplified version called time-driven ABC (see "Further reading" in Appendix 2).

Needless to say, IT projects do not correspond to this type of environment. The most common method for evaluating people *costs* in a project is through *time-entry*. ABC in IT is therefore only really applicable to stable production applications and services.

Accruals: enable revenue or expenses to be *recognized* before payment occurs.

If you've heard the term accruals before, it was probably associated with the year-end close, when all departments have to ensure that their unpaid invoices are booked to the *financial year* about to end. But accruals can also be used during the *financial year* to track *costs* with respect to budget, as we shall now see.

There are two types of accruals:

- Accrued revenue: revenue is *recognized* when it is earned, which most of the time is before payment is received.

- Accrued expenses: expenses are *recognized* when they are incurred, which is usually before the invoice is paid.

This form of accounting is called accrual accounting (the norm in any large company), as opposed to cash accounting (often used in small businesses), which only *recognizes* revenue and expenses when cash changes hands. Understanding cash accounting helps to appreciate the usefulness of accruals.

Cash accounting

In the following example, Fig. 6.2a shows how cost management with cash accounting results in an incorrect situation with respect to budget. Because the invoice for work incurred in January will only be paid in February (assuming payment terms of one month), the snapshot for the end of January shows zero costs. Of course, this is incorrect, because, to take an extreme example, if the project were cancelled at the end of January, the vendor would still have to be paid. Continuing with this cash-based approach, by the time we get to March, the YTD *costs* give the impression that only $220k has been spent (ie, 150+70), whereas in reality it is $470k (ie, 150+70+250).

Expense incurred	150k	70k	250k
	Jan	Feb	Mar
Invoice paid for expense 1		150k	
Invoice paid for expense 2			70k
Monthly costs (invoicing only)	0	150k	70k
YTD costs	0	150k	220k

Figure 6.2a Cost management based on cash accounting (all amounts in $)

Accrual accounting

Fig. 6.2b shows how accruals capture the true cost situation with respect to budget. January work is accrued at the end of January, thereby *recognizing* the *expense* the month it was incurred, regardless of when the invoice is eventually paid. By the time we get to March, the YTD *costs* are correctly shown as $470k (ie 150+70+250).

Accruals can be thought of as "pre-booked *actuals*" pending payment, thus enabling more meaningful financial reporting. They are reversed once payment has occurred.

In accounting software systems, accruals can be generated after the corresponding goods or services have been *received*.

Expense incurred	150k	70k	250k
	Jan	Feb	Mar
Accrual for expense 1	150k	-150k	
Invoice paid for expense 1		150k	
Accrual for expense 2		70k	-70k
Invoice paid for expense 2			70k
Accrual for expense 3			250k
Monthly costs (invoicing *and* accruals)	150k	70k	250k
YTD costs	150k	220k	470k

Figure 6.2b Cost management based on accrual accounting (all amounts in $)

In this simple example, invoices are submitted quickly and paid one month later; in the real world, they could be submitted late and paid late. Without accruals, therefore, your financial reporting would not only be inaccurate, but it could also become unpredictable because it is based on when vendors submit their invoices (surprisingly, not always on time) and when these invoices are eventually paid (dependent on payment terms and on process inefficiencies).

Accruals vs commitments

The alternative to using accruals to track uninvoiced work is to use *commitments* instead, which is simply uninvoiced work recorded in the *management accounting system*. An accrual goes one step further and records the *commitment* in the *financial accounting system*.

The big advantage of an accrual is that once it is recorded, it is "on the *books*", and relieves you of the burden of tracking the *commitment* through to when the invoice is eventually paid – with the attendant risk of double-counting, ie recording both the *commitment* and the paid invoice against your budget.

Actuals: short for actual *costs* incurred, as opposed to planned or budgeted *costs*.

Amortization: the technical term for the *depreciation* of non-material or intangible *assets* like patents, trademarks or brands.

Asset: tangible or intangible things that are directly or indirectly able to generate revenue over several years, thus allowing a company to produce goods or services. An asset therefore has a monetary value and can be sold if required. Tangible assets are usually called *fixed assets*, and include things like plant, property or equipment. Examples of intangible assets include things like patents and brands.

Balance sheet: A snapshot of a company's value at a specific point in time. It contains two parts, *assets* (cash, accounts receivable, equipment…) and *liabilities* (accounts payable and other debt). The difference between the two is the company's net worth (also known as owner's *equity* or shareholder's *equity*).

Because IT is so capital-intensive (up to 50% of a company's capital expenditure), it can form a significant part of the balance sheet.

An analogy would be one's personal balance sheet, which would list one's *assets* (car, savings, wife's house and jewellery…) and *liabilities* (loans, dubious investment schemes, alimony payments to first wife …).

Note that the balance sheet does not tell us how the company is performing in terms of revenue and expenses each month – that is the role of the *Income Statement* or *P&L* (of which the analogy would be your monthly salary and living expenses).

Books: see *General Accounting System*

Bottom line: the last line of the *P&L* or *Income Statement*, which represents net income – ie, sales minus total costs.

Capex: see *Costs*

Capital costs: see *Costs*

Cashflow: the difference between income and expenses. Even if revenue and profits are up, what ultimately counts in the short term is a positive cashflow – ie, money in the bank – to pay employee salaries and vendor invoices. Hence the adage "Turnover is vanity, profit is sanity, cashflow is king".

Cash out: the sum of *capex* and *opex*.

Commitments: the amount owed to a vendor once a product or a service has been delivered but the invoice has not yet been paid.

Note that a commitment is not the same as an *accrual*. Commitments are recorded in the *management accounting system*, whereas accruals are recorded in the *financial accounting system* – and are therefore officially "on the *books*".

Some companies extend the scope of commitments to include the total cost of a PO, minus the notice period for cancellation. So if a PO for six months of services can be cancelled with a notice period of one month, then commitments would be the sum of all uninvoiced work plus one month of invoicing. Needless to say, only the uninvoiced work actually done can be accrued.

Costs: Costs can be categorized in different ways.

The most fundamental cost categories are fixed costs and variable costs:

- *Fixed costs*: these are costs not directly influenced by business activity or usage – eg, rent or annual software maintenance. Fixed costs are generally easy to plan and to manage, but they are risky in that they represent long-term commitments and therefore need to be entered into with caution.

- *Variable costs:* these are costs that vary with business activity, or usage, such as telecoms charges or disk storage. Because variable costs are usually driven by decisions or events outside of IT control – eg, changes in BU usage policies, or a peak in customer service activity following a product launch – they are more difficult to plan and manage.

Fixed and variable costs are useful from an overall perspective in terms of pricing and negotiations, but they don't help in understanding who or what is driving the totals. It is therefore useful to be able to assign these costs directly or indirectly to a customer or an activity, so as to help justify IT expenditure, facilitate pricing or explore opportunities for cheaper alternatives:

- *Direct costs:* these are the portions of the fixed or variable costs that can be directly attributed to a cost centre, activity or customer. Examples include dedicated hardware, software or application support costs.

- *Indirect costs:* these are the portions of the fixed or variable costs that cannot be directly attributed to a cost centre or an activity – eg, shared infrastructure and network services. Such costs have to be apportioned or allocated based on criteria like number of users or BU revenue.

All costs, fixed or variable, direct or indirect, are ultimately classified as either capital costs or operational costs:

- *Capital costs:* more commonly known as *capex* (short for capital expenditure), this represents the substantial *assets* of the company, like plant, property, equipment – and IT systems. Capital costs figure in the balance sheet the year in which the *asset* is acquired, and are *depreciated* as expenses in the *P&L* during its useful life. *Capex* in essence pushes out expenditure incurred today to subsequent years, thus making the current year look "better" (which is why most CIOs like it…). It is therefore closely monitored by the CFO, lenders and financial markets – eg, via the *capex*-to-sales ratio – though clearly not closely enough to prevent a major telco of creative accounting fame from incorrectly capitalizing $3.8b of expenses to make its 2001 and 2002 numbers look better (what has the WorldCom to…?).

- *Operational costs:* more commonly known as *opex* (short for operational expenditure), this represents day-to-day running expenses whose effects can be measured within a short timeframe. Unlike an *asset*, an operational expense has no intrinsic value. It's just that – a one-time expense. When companies go through a round of cost-cutting as explained at the start of Chapter 1, it's usually the *opex* that's being cut. This is what the CIO monitors closely each month in the IT financial reporting.

There are clear rules for what can be capitalized and what must remain an operating expense. This is explained in detail in Chapter 2 (Budgeting rules for *capex* vs *opex*).

The sum of *capex* and *opex* is called cash out, which is the "real money" that the company has to pay for goods and services, regardless of how it will be accounted for later.

Depreciation: the reduction in value of an *asset* over its useful life (usually several years) through usage or obsolescence.

There are several methods of depreciation, the simplest of which is the linear or straight-line method, which divides the cost equally across the lifetime of the *asset*. So a $90k server with a useful life of 3 years will have an annual depreciation of $30k.

The financial impact on IT *costs* of mixing up *capex* and *opex* should hopefully be clear. If the server is correctly capitalized, the IT department will incur no *costs* this year against the IT budget; instead it will be charged $30k per year for 3 years starting next year. If, however, the *PO* incorrectly assigns the purchase to an *opex* account, then the $90k would figure as a current-year cost and hit the IT budget.

Or, to use a less obvious example, if a development team inadvertently enters $90k worth of *time entry* against functional design (*opex*) instead of technical design (*capex*), then instead of being depreciated as part of a software *asset* from next year on, the $90k would figure as a current-year cost.

Very important: depreciation is *not* a cost in terms of money out of the bank! The cost is what the company paid to acquire the *asset* (in cash or through borrowing). Depreciation is an accounting exercise that allocates a portion of the *asset*'s cost to the current financial year. The term expense in "depreciation expense" does not refer to a cost, but to *operating expense*, or *opex*. (Confused? Don't worry, so was I not too long ago!).

Direct costs: see *Costs*

EBITDA: Earnings Before Interest, Taxes, *Depreciation* and *Amortization*. This represents the first part of the *P&L* (Profit & Loss) or *Income Statement*.

In plain English, EBITDA is operating profit, which is sales minus operating *costs* – ie, the day-to-day running *costs* like sales, marketing and administration. But plain English doesn't help the non-specialist to understand what the remaining *costs* are, and that's where EBITDA comes in:

<u>P&L or *Income Statement*</u>

Sales (*top line*)

- operating costs

EBITDA (operating profit)

- Depreciation

- Amortization

EBIT (operating income)

- Interest

EBT (earnings before taxes)

- Taxes

Net Income (*bottom line*)

So, you might ask, why bother with EBITDA? Why not just go straight to the net income at the *bottom line*? The main reason is to be able to compare the performance of companies in different sectors: because some industries are more capital-intensive than others, subtracting *depreciation* expenses would distort comparisons. EBITDA is therefore only useful for companies with large amounts of *fixed assets*, which generate large *depreciation* charges (like telcos or manufacturing companies).

Finally, because EBITDA was often misunderstood by investors before the dot-bomb crash in 2001 as representing *cashflow* – a misconception that companies didn't exactly go out of their way to correct – EBITDA also became known as Earnings Before I Trick Dumb Auditors!

Equity: the difference between *assets* and *liabilities*. Equity can be owner's equity or shareholder's equity. Also known as net worth.

Expenses: Operating expenses or *opex*. Sometimes used as a verb, as in "expensed".

Financial accounting system: see *General accounting system*

Financial year (FY): the annual 12-month period over which a company does business, which may or may not coincide with the calendar year of January to December. The financial year is divided into 12 *fiscal periods* and 4 quarters.

At the end of each quarter, publicly traded companies publish their quarterly results, and at the end of the financial year close their *books* and declare their financial results.

Fiscal period: see *Financial Year*

Fiscal year: see *Financial Year*

Fixed assets: see *Assets*.

Fixed costs: see *Costs*

Forecast: actuals plus estimated remaining costs. The forecast is in essence a revised budget, based on better visibility on what's really happening and is likely to happen next. The original budget will often have been defined at least six months beforehand, based on assumptions and estimates that almost always have to be adjusted as reality sets in.

A forecast should cover, at the very minimum, the rest of the financial year and, ideally, a rolling 12-month period (called a rolling forecast).

GAAP (Generally Accepted Accounting Principles): the rules and guidelines for financial accounting, used mainly in the US.

In a globalized world however, there is now increasing convergence towards IFRS (International Financial Reporting Standards), used in Europe and the rest of the world. The US Securities and Exchange Commission (SEC) has set preliminary dates for the conversion, saying that US publicly-traded companies will need to use IFRS from 2014 onwards.

General Accounting System (GAS): the company's official system of record from a legal and regulatory perspective. It comprises a collection of accounts or *chart of accounts* that covers *assets, liabilities, equity,* revenue and *expenses*. It is from the GAS that financial statements are prepared for debtors, creditors, lenders and financial markets.

Also known as *the financial accounting system* or *the books* or the *general ledger*.

GASs don't have the level of detail required to manage IT projects and applications, hence the need for *Management Accounting Systems*.

General ledger (GL): see *General accounting system*

IFRS (International Financial Reporting Standards): see *GAAP*

Income statement: a company financial statement that shows the difference between revenue and *costs* – in other words, income. Also known as the *P&L*. The income statement shows the financial performance of the company, in other words, whether it made or lost money over a specific period.

Note that the income statement represents profit and loss over a specific period (usually a month), unlike the *balance sheet*, which is a snapshot of the company's value at a point in time.

An analogy would be one's personal income statement, which would list one's revenue (salary and other earnings) and expenses (car payments, restaurant bills, alimony …).

The most common format of the income statement in the corporate world is *EBITDA*.

Indirect costs: see *Costs*

Liabilities: a company's obligations to its creditors.

Management Accounting System (MAS): a parallel accounting system that augments the *general accounting system*. It manages *costs* and revenue based on management criteria like projects, applications or customers. Unlike the *general accounting system*, a MAS does not need to comply with legal or regulatory requirements – but if the latter feeds the former, it must be possible to demonstrate how the final numbers were arrived at.

MASs can vary from Excel spreadsheets and *time entry* systems all the way to PPM or ITFM systems.

NPV (Net Present Value): The present value (discounted at the required rate of return) of an investment's future *cashflows* minus the initial investment. An NPV of zero means that the project pays for the original investment plus the required rate of return. A positive NPV means a better return, and a negative NPV a worse return.

NPV is a financial criterion for evaluating the profitability of a project investment. Note, though, that there are also other, non-financial, criteria for evaluating project investments (see "Combining *costs* and benefits" in Chapter 3)

Operational costs: see *Costs*.

Opex: see *Costs*.

P&L (Profit and Loss): see *Income Statement*.

Portfolio Management: an investment method that spreads investments across a number of well-defined categories based on a combination of business objectives, expected return and risk (see "Portfolio-based investment planning" in Chapter 2). The layman's equivalent of portfolio management is "don't put all of your eggs in one basket".

Purchase order (PO): an official request to a vendor to provide goods or services at agreed conditions (price, quantity, delivery dates and payment terms).

It is important from an IT cost-management perspective to correctly determine whether the goods or services being purchased are to be assigned to a *capex* or an *opex* account, or a combination of the two. ERP systems can be automatically set up to do this for unambiguous things like physical goods (eg servers = capex). Unfortunately, this is not always possible for services delivered by contractors, consulting companies or integrators, which can be capex or opex. In such cases then, this has to be manually done.

Purchase requisition: a request to raise a purchase order (*PO*) as part of an approval process. An approved purchase requisition normally contains all of the information necessary to raise the *PO*.

Receiving: the accounting process whereby the goods or services associated with a *PO* are recorded as having been delivered. Since most IT purchases are for services and for people (contractors and consultants) rather than physical goods in an inventory or stock environment, receiving usually means entering the number of days people have worked (time and materials) or the monetary amount corresponding to a project milestone payment (fixed-price contract).

In accounting software systems, once goods or services have been received, *accruals* can be generated.

Recognition: the financial term used to signify that an income or an *expense* is "real" from an accounting perspective. Under *accrual* accounting, a company can recognize revenue once it has sold a product or delivered a service, even though it has not yet been paid.

But there are exceptions. For example, if a SaaS vendor (that normally invoices clients for monthly usage) negotiates a contract in which the client pays the first year's subscription upfront, then it can only recognize 1/12th of this amount each month, even though the entire one-year amount is sitting in its coffers. Another example would be an integrator working on a high-value, fixed-price ERP project; because of the risk associated with this type of project, the integrator might decide to only partially recognize milestone payments already received, and wait till the end of the project before recognizing the full amount.

The proverb "don't count your chickens before they are hatched" is the farmer's equivalent of revenue recognition.

Just as for revenue, *accrual* accounting allows for *costs* to be recognized when they are incurred, even though the invoice has not yet been paid (see Fig. 6.2b for an example).

Rolling forecast: see *Forecast*

Sunk costs: previously incurred *costs* that are unrecoverable. Usually associated with *writing off* an investment.

TCO (Total Cost of Ownership): total lifetime costs, from "cradle to grave", comprising both acquisition *costs* and ongoing *operational costs*. In the absence of TCO, people may focus incorrectly – by accident or design – on either the acquisition *costs* ("it only *costs* this much …") or the ongoing *costs* ("look how low the running *costs* are…"), especially when this also includes hidden costs.

The concept of TCO first gained notoriety in IT when Gartner introduced the concept in 1978 to demonstrate that for a desktop computer, the initial price tag accounted for an average of only 20% of the total lifetime costs, with the rest consumed by administration, training and support.

Time entry: a method of capturing the time people spend on tasks or activities, which can be translated into *costs* and then assigned to projects, applications and services. In addition, each task or activity can be assigned to *capex* or *opex*, as required by financial accounting rules.

Top line: the first line of the *P&L* or *Income Statement*, which is sales or revenue.

Variable costs: see *Costs*

Write off: to reduce the value of an *asset* to zero by charging it to *expense* or loss, resulting in the *asset* being removed from the *books*. So, if an IT system were decommissioned after only a few years, it would have to be written off.

A write-down is a partial write-off of an *asset*, to account for a reduction in its value while still remaining on the *books*.

Important: a write-off is not "free"! To take a simple analogy, if you suddenly decide you can no longer afford your monthly car payments over the next 5 years, you know you're going to have to pay the outstanding instalments. Similarly, cancelling a project or decommissioning a system before the end of its useful life can have significant financial impact, because outstanding *depreciation* expenses have to be written off. In other words, the now worthless *asset* is removed from the *balance sheet* and recorded as an *expense* against the current period's *P&L*.

A write-off can have unintended consequences on current year expenses. Staying with the car example, paying off 5 years of outstanding instalments all at once will represent a huge, unplanned expense for that year – and you'll probably have to cut down on other discretionary expenses, such as vacation.

Similarly, cancelling a failed $1m IT project one year after launch would result in the IT budget taking a big hit. If the project was supposed to be straight-line depreciated over 5 years, then the annual cost against the IT budget is only supposed to be $200k. If instead it is now cancelled in year 2, then the IT budget would end up taking a hit to the tune of $800k (years 2-5)! The IT department might then have to cut down on other expenses – eg, postpone or even cancel some other project in order to pay for the cancelled project.

So, paradoxically, cancelling a project soon after depreciation has started might save money in the long run (by not providing ongoing funding to an application with a poor return on investment), but in the year of its cancellation, it would end up costing money!

Appendix 2

Further Reading

ARTICLES AND REPORTS

- "Accounting for Software Development Costs", by Paul Munter, CPA Journal.

- "Budgeting – Chargeback for good or evil", by Malcolm Wheatley, on CIO.com.

- "Capex vs Opex: most people miss the point about cloud economics", by Bernard Golden, on CIO.com.

- "Chargebacks and Information Technology Funding", by Philip J. Goldstein, at EDUCAUSE Center for Applied Research.

- "Creating and Operating an Effective and Equitable Shared Services Chargeback Framework", Accenture (2004).

- "Market Overview: IT Financial Management Software", by Thomas Mendel and Peter O'Neill, Forrester (2009).

- "No Crystal Ball for IT", by Harvard Professor Rob Austin, on CIO.com.

- "The real cost of failed projects", by Ilya Bogorad, on www.projectsmart.co.uk.

- "Time-Driven Activity-Based Costing", by Robert S. Kaplan and Steven R. Anderson (2003).

BOOKS

- "FINANCIAL ACCOUNTING – A Mercifully Brief Introduction", by Michael Sack Elmaleh (2005). Epiphany Communications.

- "IT FINANCIAL MANAGEMENT", by Maxime Sottini (2009). VHP.

- "IT SUCCESS!– Towards a New Model for Information Technology", by Michael Gentle (2007). Wiley.

- "THE INTERNAL ECONOMY" by N. Dean Meyer (2004). NDMA.

WEBSITES

- www.accountingcoach.com (Accounting Coach).

- www.investorwords.com (Investor Words).

- www.itfma.com (The IT Financial Management Association).

- www.understand-accounting.net (Understand Accounting).

24797482R00081

Made in the USA
Lexington, KY
01 August 2013